W9-CHZ-264

WILD HABITATS

Aleta Karstad's
WILD
HABITATS

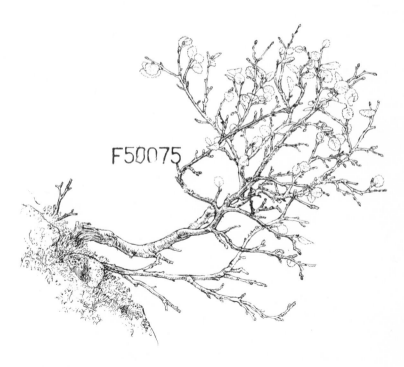

F50075

Charles Scribner's Sons
New York

For Francis and Grandma, whose books had to wait,
and in fond memory of Paul W. Schueler.

WILD HABITATS

Copyright © Aleta Karstad, 1979
All rights reserved. No part of this book may be reproduced in any form without
the permission of Charles Scribner's Sons.

1 3 5 7 9 11 13 15 17 19 I/C 20 18 16 14 12 10 8 6 4 2

Printed in Canada

Library of Congress Catalog Card Number 78-78336

SBN 0-684-16236-9

Contents

Foreword

As this manuscript goes to the publisher, home has been Toronto for eight months. All winter I've stood on the corner outside as a school crosswalk guard, and Fred has walked daily some four or five miles to the University to use the computer. Indoors Aleta has stuck to the task of writing from notes and illustrating from slides and collections. Books are piled everywhere, including the kitchen table.

We are five individuals (two cats and three people) who travelled in two vans for a year and a half. Fred and Aleta are married. From coast to coast, out of doors, through all seasons, we drew, made listings and tables and notes, photographed, pressed and boxed, and stuffed into bottles all manner of things. Crisscrossing the continent twice, we seldom drove more than 100 miles in a day. We mostly burned wood, and we ate all the foods we could find.

The task of writing the words and painting and drawing the pictures that make up this book was Aleta's. She wrote notes on folded-up file cards and hoarded her bits and scraps of description until enough was collected for a chapter. The art work was not so convenient. Sometimes specimens could be taken for later, but most of the time she found no alternative to illustrating in the field. Aleta copies light and draws directly from nature. It only takes part of her mind, but requires her constant attention; often for quite a long time. To keep her mind occupied, we often would read to her. To save time, she worked to size, or only 10 percent up.

Thoreau maintained that one could come to know the world in two ways; go around it, or observe it as it passes through one's own garden. We have tried to do both. With households in storage, we lived in the open, working and resting and recreating in places described in this book. Many observations occurred by accident, while cooking or bathing, or watching the sun set. Each locality was explored of necessity, and quickly became quite familiar. We often stayed long enough to make friends and neighbors of "locals," and in so doing became local ourselves.

I remember back before I got involved with this book. I was hoping to write one much like it myself. I felt that I really needed a transportable volume of descriptions and illustration of out-of-doors North America. I was planning to go to Australia and Asia, and wanted a book to read (in case I should get stuck in the Calcutta Railway Station).

For the three of us, home is a continent large. We've had a lot of garden to explore and we know that a lot of it is not in this book. However, for most Canadians and Americans, it should be possible to find one's own habitat within these covers and explore it further from there.

Franklin D. Ross
Toronto, 20 April 1978

Preface

In this book I have tried to illustrate plants and animals that live together in different parts of temperate and boreal North America. This project has its roots in my longstanding habit of bringing things home to draw. Before a drawing looks anything like its subject, the illustrator must understand its structure. Because I learn so much while drawing in detail, I feel that I can never see a thing as clearly as when I have drawn or painted it. When I am in a habitat, describing it in words works in much the same way: In perceiving beauty and order I feel an urge to capture it.

One of the main difficulties in writing the book was first to decide what kinds of habitats to describe, and then whether something I was looking at qualified as part of one of my habitats. In most cases it did, since most habitats grade into others, and many species are shared among them.

As I retype these chapters I am struck by differences in the way I presented them. Some seem to be leisurely guided strolls, while in others I seem to insist upon dragging you through the whys and wherefores of nearly everything I see, but I had neither room nor time to describe and draw as much as I would have liked in each place.

I have named the habitats only as they appeared to me, and as useful handles on kinds of places; I did not intend to make any rules about what certain ecological communities should properly be called. I have seen each habitat as being characterized or unified by some factor, and the unifying principles vary among habitats. Sometimes a chapter describes an entire natural landscape, and sometimes only a small part or a particular aspect of an area. As most of my material was obtained by direct observation rather than by library work, a struggle for consistency in organization would have made this a much more formal work. I have capitalized the common names of species because they are proper nouns and could otherwise be confused with description.

During the making of this book, we have revisited old familiar places and have learned new things, and in exploring strange habitats, have come to love them. We hope you too will recognize familiar lives and places, and also be delighted by new ones.

I thank the many kind people who have helped us during our travels, and who have given much encouragement in their interest and enthusiasm for the book. I hope I have done justice to something of the natural history of their own special areas. I am grateful for the help of the curators and staff of the National Museum of Natural Sciences, the Royal Ontario Museum, and the University of Toronto Botany Department, who helped with the identification of plants and animals. I especially appreciate the time and patience taken by Soren Bondrup-Nielsen, E.L. Bousfield, J. Hodgins, J.D. Rising, and Trudy Rising in critically reading the manuscript. Of course, Fred, Frank, and Francis and Joyce Cook have been helpful and supportive in more ways than could be mentioned.

Aleta Karstad

Ocean Beach

Ocean beaches are narrow margins of unstable material: sand, mud, or small stones which are shifted by the water. This chapter is based on beach, dunes, and salt marsh at Cap Lumière, New Brunswick, and beaches at St. Andrews, New Brunswick; and Qualicum Beach and Tofino, Vancouver Island, British Columbia.

Rushing forward and hissing back, waves of salt water tumble sand grains and raft strands of seaweed. The beach is a movable shoreline. Sand is always being washed away from some stretches of beach and piled on others, following the rising and falling tides, and the direction and force of waves. In some places it accumulates as barriers across the mouths of bays. Finer particles settle behind these barriers and form the mud on which the grasses of the salt marsh grow; while along the open beaches the wind blows the sand up beyond the reach of the water to form dunes between beach and marsh.

A group of Sanderlings sprint ahead of you along the beach. They stop frequently to poke deftly in the sand with their long, stout black bills in search of small crustaceans and burrowing worms, and run ahead again on a quick blur of neat black legs. They turn their heads from side to side, looking back at you, first with one bright eye, then with the other.

In an irregular line along the beach, drifts of glistening seaweeds and Eelgrass mark the farthest reach of the waves at the last high tide. Older drift lines, higher on the beach, are partially covered by windblown sand. Here the Eelgrass is bleached and thin, lying in tangled piles, and the rockweed *Fucus* is dried to tough black scraps. Old bird carcasses are mounds of sand, marked by ragged feathers and a few white bones. While fresh, this material was sorted and picked at by gulls and crows, and when seaweed and carcasses began to be buried by sand, they were chewed by countless beach fleas. The most terrestrial of the marine amphipods, these small crustaceans jump and scramble for cover by the hundreds when you turn over a damp tangle of stranded ocean plant life.

Rolls and scrolls of glossy fresh kelp fronds are pushed and dragged by the frothy wave margins which lap the firm sand. A long, slim kelp stipe lies coiled like a smooth rope. It ends in a fistlike holdfast, still clutching a big deepwater Horse Mussel whose byssus threads were broken when the kelp was wrenched back and forth by the strong surf of the last storm.

A brittle white sponge, worn by the sand, looks like a small egg-shaped lump of coral nestled in a scramble of darkening Eelgrass. Long, soft, yellow sponges, ragged and shredded from the battering of waves, lie limply about. A small beige and purple Quahog shell is perforated by a neat round hole drilled by a hungry moon snail. The shells on the beach are being ground into particles smaller than sand grains, and their calcium will be dissolved in the seawater. A piece of olive green *Fucus*, far from its rocky holdfast, bears the dull, whitish honeycomb pattern of the base of a once thriving bryozoan colony. A rock crab lies on its back, the sand around it patterned by gull tracks. Most of its meat has already been taken. Here and there on the sand are tight ruffles of dark red Irish Moss, and thin, translucent, brick red leaves of Dulse. Both are edible. They are salty, and slightly crunchy, with the flavor of an ocean breeze; they are also good dried.

Where the beach slope is gradual, the sand grains pile up against each other as each wave slips back toward the sea, and the water digs a trough behind each little drift. In this way, the waves leave elaborate repeating patterns, infinitely variable according to the angle and direction of the slope, sand grain size, and the force of the waves. The subtle way in which the patterns change is a lesson in design, and when the tide goes out the beach surface is firmly water-sculpted, with interlocking sand ridges and valleys for as far as you can see. On this background run the "tractor tread" tracks of small crabs, and the definite, wandering grooves left by travelling dog whelks. Slight mounds, topped by long, curly sand castings are plentiful in some places, where a careful shovel can turn out a hefty pink and red lugworm with a row of

Murre, *Uria aalge*, dead on beach. A deepwater diving bird, killed by oil. Green Point, Long Beach, Vancouver Island, B.C. February 1977

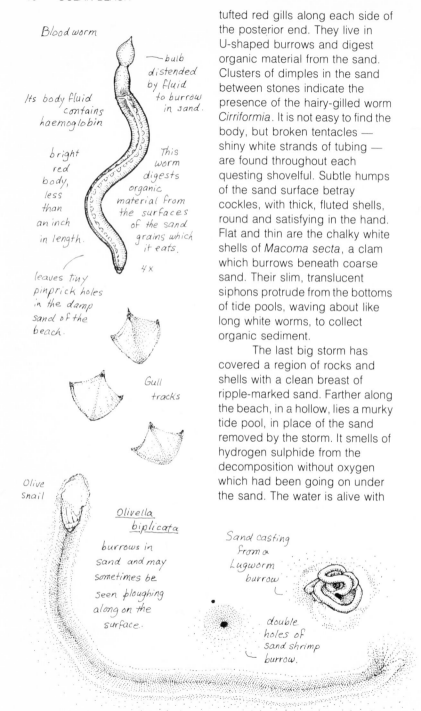

Blood worm

Its body fluid contains haemoglobin

bulb distended by fluid to burrow in sand.

bright red body, less than an inch in length.

This worm digests organic material from the surfaces of the sand grains which it eats.

4 x

leaves tiny pinprick holes in the damp sand of the beach.

Gull tracks

Olive Snail

Olivella biplicata

burrows in sand and may sometimes be seen ploughing along on the surface.

Sand casting from a Lugworm burrow

double holes of sand shrimp burrow.

tufted red gills along each side of the posterior end. They live in U-shaped burrows and digest organic material from the sand. Clusters of dimples in the sand between stones indicate the presence of the hairy-gilled worm *Cirriformia*. It is not easy to find the body, but broken tentacles — shiny white strands of tubing — are found throughout each questing shovelful. Subtle humps of the sand surface betray cockles, with thick, fluted shells, round and satisfying in the hand. Flat and thin are the chalky white shells of *Macoma secta*, a clam which burrows beneath coarse sand. Their slim, translucent siphons protrude from the bottoms of tide pools, waving about like long white worms, to collect organic sediment.

The last big storm has covered a region of rocks and shells with a clean breast of ripple-marked sand. Farther along the beach, in a hollow, lies a murky tide pool, in place of the sand removed by the storm. It smells of hydrogen sulphide from the decomposition without oxygen which had been going on under the sand. The water is alive with gammarids and little sculpins, flitting and darting, finding lots of food in this new place. A Great Blue Heron's tracks are left in the unsettled sand where it was fishing a moment before you came.

Many animals which must hide from predators during daylight become active in the open after dark. Exploring the beach with a lantern can reveal Clam Worms crawling like long, wiggly, iridescent Chinese dragons. They hunt over the wet mud for small worms and crustaceans, and their bodies lash back and forth in fluid S shapes as they swim in the tide pools. Moon snails glide with ominous rapidity across the bottom with their mantles folded up over the edges of their large round shells. When one of them finds a clam it bores through the shell, and feeds on the body within. The small, pale Mudflat Crab, *Hemigrapsis oregonensis*, runs about, scavenging on the high mud beaches at night. Another scavenger, the brown mudsnail *Nassarius* creeps over the surface in search of food, tasting the sand with its short black proboscis. Often they congregate to feast on dead fish. A thin jet of water squirting from the mud may show where you step close to the siphon of a Soft-shelled Clam, *Mya arenaria*, which lives more than a shell-length down in mud. The horny-plated siphons of *Tresus*, the giant Horse Clams, also squirt as they retract from disturbance. Half a meter below, their big bodies, barely covered with shell, sit firmly wedged in the mud. They look like

Aerial view of intergradation of habitats at Cap Lumière, Richibuctu, N.B. October 1977

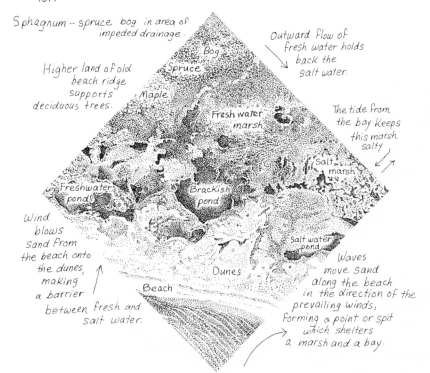

Sphagnum – spruce bog in area of impeded drainage.

Bog

Spruce

Higher land of old beach ridge supports deciduous trees.

Maple

Outward flow of fresh water holds back the salt water.

Fresh water marsh

The tide from the bay keeps this marsh salty

Salt marsh

Freshwater pond

Brackish pond

Wind blows sand from the beach onto the dunes, making a barrier between fresh and salt water.

Salt water pond

Dunes

Beach

Waves move sand along the beach in the direction of the prevailing winds, forming a point or spit which shelters a marsh and a bay.

giant *Mya*, but are more closely related to the hard-shelled surf clams of the sandy beach.

It isn't possible for plants to find roothold among the sharp-edged, shifting grains of a sandy beach, but in softer, muddier sand Eelgrass can grow below the tide level. Above mid-tide, in the Atlantic salt marsh, the salt grasses *Spartina* bind the mud into a continuous sod with their roots and rhizomes. Small, high-spired, checkered periwinkles *Littorina saxatilis*, feed on diatoms and algae at the grass bases. Coarse-leaved *Spartina alternifolia* grow in tall swaths along the edges of the creeks that fill and drain the marsh with each tide. Their tough bases are strong against tidal currents. The narrow-leaved *Spartina patens* grow on higher tidal flats in a dense sod of dead leaves and stems which accumulate over the years to form the salt marsh peat.

Because it is alternately wet and dry, hot and cold, and salt and fresh, few animals live in the salt marsh mat. With time, the old leaves break down and wash out to sea as a rich detritus, food for marine life of the bay. The *Spartina* grasses have a high requirement for iron, which is brought in abundance by every tide, and which fixes with a sulphide in the mud. The oxygen which the grass carries in its hollow roots not only enables the roots to breathe while buried in the marsh mud, but also combines with the mud's sulphide to free the iron for use by the plant. *Spartina* secretes salt through the pores of its leaves to reduce its internal salt level.

When you walk on the thick, springy bed of the weak-stemmed *Spartina patens*, all pushed down by the wind and tide in broad, swirled patterns, the peat gives slightly beneath each step, and the grass seems

Cobbled beach scene: Shore Crab, *Hemigrapsis nudus*, Limpet, *Acmaea*, barnacles, *Balanus glandula*, Blue Mussel, *Mytilus edulis*, and Eelgrass, *Zostera marina*. Boundary Bay, Tsawwassen, B.C. 21 October 1976

like the thick, hairy pelt of a giant, fat-backed buffalo. Toothed cinquefoil leaves spread like the fingers of hands at the ends of long thin stems lying flat with the grass. Sprigs of Sea Lavender stand, stiff and upright, their branching stems misted with tiny pinkish flowers. Short-stemmed Seaside Goldenrod pokes stiffly from the grass, topped with a golden froth of fluffy bloom. Bushy saltworts grow in wet places by holding so much salt in their tissues that seawater cannot draw the water from their succulent stems. These are Sea Blite, *Atriplex*, and glassworts *Salicornia*, which are edible, salty, and slightly acid to the taste. The seeds of most marsh plants require the fresh water of spring rains to begin growth, but *Salicornia* seeds may even germinate in water that is saltier than seawater.

The smooth undulations of sand dune crests break the horizon as you look from the salt marsh toward the open ocean. The wind has blown hills of sand up from the beach, and your way toward the sea may be an obstacle course of brackish ponds, meadows of grasses and sedges, low grassy dunes, pockets of dense Bayberry scrub, and perhaps even freshwater ponds, above the salt groundwater within the sand, and isolated from high ocean tides by the barrier of dunes.

The tops of the low inner dunes are gray and crusty with *Cladonia* lichens that cake the surface of the sand and retain moisture at the surface for a while after each rain. Leathery, dark

The Glasswort,
Salicornia, in salt marsh

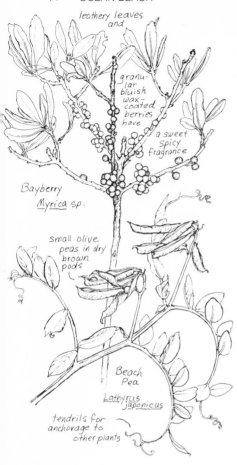

leathery leaves
and

granu-
lar
bluish
wax-
coated
berries
have

a sweet
spicy
fragrance

Bayberry

Myrica sp.

small olive
peas in dry
brown
pods

Beach
Pea

Lathyrus
japonicus

tendrils for
anchorage to
other plants

green Bearberry stretches trailing strands, rooting where it can. Little earth star puffballs seem like scraps of litter on the sand, along with the crab parts and mussel shells dropped on the dunes by the gulls. On the backsides of these rounded, stable dunes, protected from sharp, windblown sand, are low, sprawling, gray-green bushes of the Golden Heather *Hudsonia* and a few meandering, oval-leaved vines of Beach Pea, tightly winding their tendrils about anything more solid than sand.

Beach Pea also grows among the strong stems of Dune Grass which waves long, pale golden flower spikes like flexible spears from the crests of the high line of barrier dunes that face the sea. The wind blows sand up from the beach, over and through this grass, splitting the tips of old leaves into hairlike shreds; grains of sand are constantly shifting and drifting between the grass bases. Last year's grass leaves crisscross over the sand, trapping some of it to build the dune higher. If you grasp one of the thick stems and tug, it will pull up abruptly, broken off where it narrows to a blunt base. If you dig into the sand between grasses with your hands you can feel the hard yellow rhizomes, taut between grass plants, holding the dune together underground like a network of cables. Fine roots run into the sand from thickened joints every few centimetres along their lengths. When motor vehicles are driven over the dunes, their weight breaks the rhizomes of the Dune Grass and the wind gouges a bowl-shaped blowout, spreading tons of sand over the delicate desert gardens of the inner dunes, and choking the edge of the salt marsh.

Eastern Rainforest

Exceptionally humid forest habitats occur patchily in the east: at higher elevations of the Adirondacks and Appalachians, on the coast of Maine, the Maritime provinces, and Quebec, and on the coasts and valleys of Newfoundland. This chapter is based on such forests in southern New Brunswick; central Gaspé Peninsula; and western Newfoundland.

The terrain of the eastern rainforest has withstood the repeated grinding of the Ice Ages. The trees which grow here are not the special giant species of the west coast rainforest, whose mountain slopes have never been completely covered by ice. Rather, White Spruce, Balsam Fir, and Paper Birch are ordinary boreal forest species, grown extra large on the mild, wet border of the Atlantic.

    When you have pushed through the bushes, passed the saplings at the edge, and come into the forest dimness, go a little farther. Twist and turn among close-standing spruce and fir. Walk along one mossy horizontal tree trunk, and crawl under the next. You breathe the breath of mosses and ferns, trees and fungi, cool and damp, a little fresh and a little earthy. The scent of resin and the close heaviness of rotting logs hangs in the air all around you. The gentle hushing sound of the wind in the upper branches is occasionally pierced by the clear music of an unseen kinglet or the hoarse voices of a pair of Ravens conversing as they pass somewhere above.

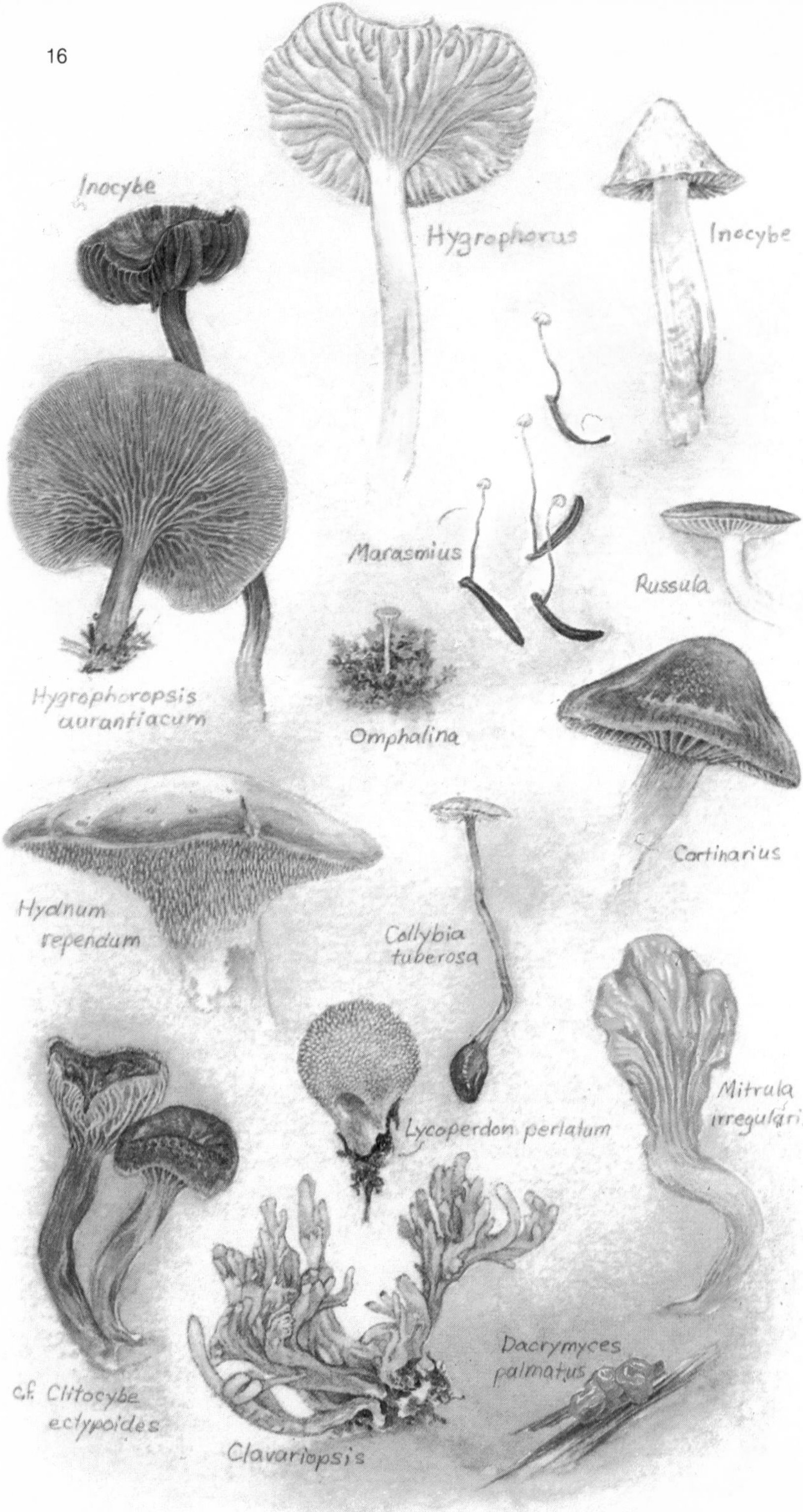

Inocybe

Hygrophorus

Inocybe

Marasmius

Russula

Hygrophoropsis
aurantiacum

Omphalina

Cortinarius

Hydnum
repandum

Collybia
tuberosa

Lycoperdon perlatum

Mitrula
irregularis

cf. Clitocybe
eclypoides

Clavariopsis

Dacrymyces
palmatus

The spruce branches are hoarfrosted with lacy lichens, and fringed and tufted with *Usnea* lichen, Old Man's Beard, clinging to twigs and branches like wisps of living fog, and moving in the faint breeze like the ghosts of trees long fallen. The mood is gloomy, even on a sunny day, and the forest, as a living being, is protective of its dim dampness and the slow quiet of its inner life.

The forest floor is soft and moist, but tough, filled with roots which gather food and water for the lives of trees, which in needlefall, death, and the leaching of the rain, sooner or later return their elements to the soil. A delicate network of threads of fungi cells is everywhere in the soil and in rotting wood. From it, mushrooms spring to shed spores from their folded expanses of gills, tubes, or pores. Many trees, young and old, have U-shaped bends in their trunks that tell of being borne down in past years by a fallen neighbor. The shape of the living tree was forever altered by some log that has now softened and fallen away, food for mushrooms and a home for centipedes. In a decade, the log over which you have stepped will no longer be there. Perhaps a cluster of woodferns will arch their fronds in that place, having risen from the fusion of spore-grown egg and sperm in the mossy pelt of the log, or a colony of small brown-capped mushrooms will spring from what was once sodden bark.

Indian Pipe rises in a close group from a mossy bed. Like the mushrooms, it lacks chlorophyll and therefore is not green. It takes its nourishment from the forest floor, and shows itself only to reproduce. In early spring, last summer's ghostly white drooping flowers are now turned upright, atop thin, stiff, brown stems. Near them, in the shelter of a rich green garden — once an old log — nestles a cluster of light, dry droppings, small, round and slightly flattened. There are so many places to hide in the rainforest that it is unlikely that you will see one, but by their droppings you know that Snowshoe Hares are in the forest with you. Perhaps one is watching you, doe-eyed and long-eared, still flecked with the white of its winter coat. It sits silent in a cave between the roots of an ancient spruce, velvet nose twitching as it waits for you to go. It wants to return to nibbling the soft, bright fiddleheads, tightly curled young leaves of *Cysopteris fragilis*, the Fragile Fern, that peek from the cracks of an old stump.

The golden-furred fiddleheads of Marginal Woodferns are unfurling. Around them, last year's leathery, yellow-green fronds lie flattened, exhausted by the winter's burden of snow, but still briefly able to photosynthesize in the early spring. The floor of the rainforest has plenty of green that has lasted through the winter. The small, round, single leaves of Kidney-leaved Buttercup and the dark green of Goldthread are sprinkled about. The ground is parasoled with the Herb Dogwood, *Cornus canadensis*, carpeted with moss, and forested in miniature with clubmosses.

As summer nears, the forest retains cool pockets of snow. These are sprinkled with bark and twigs, and melt slowly into little brooks that trickle and murmur along winding troughs and deep gullies. The music of

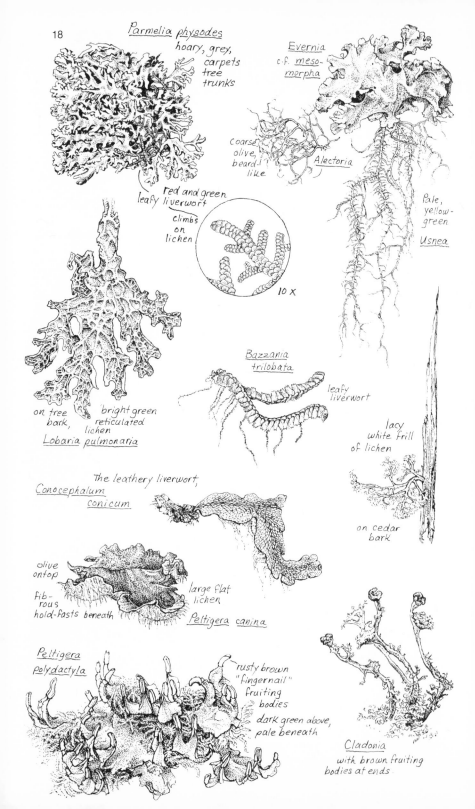

Parmelia physodes
hoary, grey,
carpets
tree
trunks

Evernia
c.f. _meso-
morpha_

coarse
olive,
beard-
like

Alectoria

Pale,
yellow-
green
Usnea

red and green
leafy liverwort

climbs
on
lichen

10 X

_Bazzania
trilobata_

leafy
liverwort

on tree
bark,
Lobaria pulmonaria

bright green
reticulated
lichen

lacy
white frill
of lichen

on cedar
bark

The leathery liverwort,
_Conocephalum
conicum_

olive
on top

fib-
rous
hold-fasts beneath

large flat
lichen
Peltigera canina

_Peltigera
polydactyla_

rusty brown
"fingernail"
fruiting
bodies

dark green above,
pale beneath

Cladonia
with brown fruiting
bodies at ends.

the rainforest stream lures you over and around shaggy logs and rocks to view gardens of delicate mosses and ferns. The damp darkness of small caverns beneath tiny waterfalls are lined with watery diamonds clinging to the hairlike tips of moss leaves. Boulders are embroidered with liverworts, and meltwater runs in dark paths of cold crystal. It disappears at your feet into the leaf mold, secretly moving through the closely woven fabric of tree roots and rootlets; then, reappearing behind you, it drops with a song of countless clear notes played in unison, from pool to pool.

This spring, melting snow uncovers large mushrooms, their caps and stems broken by the snow's weight. Some big, brown shiny-capped mushrooms look vigorous, but their time is past, and they will collapse when warm weather comes. There are fungi everywhere you look. Last fall's puffballs nestle like tiny crumpled eggs, paper-thin sacs filled with finest fluff and dustlike spores. Bracket fungi jut like brown shelves from tree trunks, and very small fungi live everywhere. Tiny black suction cups poke at you from the side of a tree, fuzzy and short-necked, but glossy inside the cups. Minute white cups, tan inside, bead the smooth branches of a spruce like the smallest of pearls. Fungi like globs of wrinkled, soft black rubber grow on trunks and logs, along with brilliant yellow-orange ones that are almost translucent, with a dry, waxy-looking surface. Low and dusty, molds fill cracks inconspicuously, and subtly coat things which are moist and dead. Molds are quick to grow and reproduce, raising their spores

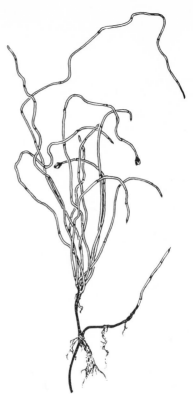

Dwarf Scouring Rush, a horsetail, *Equisetum scirpoides,* crinkly, coarse, and dark green, partly buried in wet moss. Parc de la Gaspésie, P.Q. 3 October 1977

Red Squirrel, *Tamiasciurus hudsonicus.* Parc de la Gaspésie, P.Q. 30 September 1977

Two lichens that live on tree trunks: *Icmadophila ericetorum* (left) and *Mycoblastus sanguinarius* (right). Parc de la Gaspésie, P.Q. 30 September 1977

only a few cell-heights into the air, and can use fleeting sources of food.

Lichens grow in forms almost as diverse as fungi, and live in even more diverse places. I have climbed a tall White Spruce, forcing my way up through its prickly interior, and counted a score of lichens, each kind with its place in a zonation as regular as that at the edge of the nearby sea. Tight lacy forms grow on both rocks and trees, but the misty green *Usnea* grows only on trees. You may find tiny speckles sprinkled liberally on the limbs of spruces, dainty orange pans with white, upturned rims. All around, lichens splotch tree trunks like aluminum paint, too flat and thin to show any detail. Lichens with stems, mostly of the multiform genus *Cladonia*, compete with the luxuriant mosses, and grow among them on stumps and logs in a miniature landscape: bushes of bright green moss and tall curved spikes of pale green lichen, elegant stems crowned by ruffles, and more stems growing up into saucers or funnels. Some have smooth surfaces, and some are almost scaly, or frilled and curled into chalky white parsley.

A lichen is not a single being, although it may appear so, but a fungus and an alga living together and depending on one another. The alga needs the fungus as a body, for structure and protection, and the fungus uses the products of the food-making of its green symbiont. Often one kind of alga lives with different kinds of fungi to produce various lichens, so lichens are named by the fungus, not the alga. In the host of delicate and graceful *Cladonia* before you, flaring like trumpets, branching like antlers, and spreading like lace foam, there may be a species unknown to science. The identification of lichens is a matter of chemistry, tracking down the organic acids that characterize each species, and often many kinds can appear identical to the eye.

As you push deeper into the forest, pressing past the dry, springy lower branches,

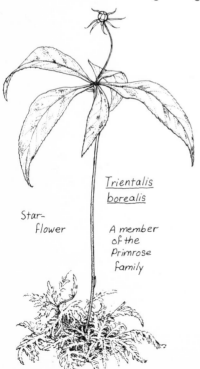

Trientalis borealis

Star-flower

A member of the Primrose family

squeezing yourself between trees, you may come face to bark with a giant old birch, a meter through the base, dead of old age, but still standing. Its thick, ragged curls of white and pink bark are rimed shaggily with thin papery lichens, and encrusted with dense crinkly ones. The great tree towers above you, its main branches long ago broken in two or three blunt directions. The larger of the limbs remain where they fell, strong tubes of bark half full of punky, moist wood chunks. Birch bark resists decay, and even in this condition, having lain on the wet ground for years, it will burn eagerly, with long, orange, crackling flames and black oily smoke.

Birch logs are a favorite habitat for snails. If a snail doesn't just happen to be hauling its round, nut-brown, finely fuzzy shell up the chalky bark, or traveling briskly, with tiny turban shell held high and periscope eyes waving, along a pendulous strand of moss, then roll the log, or tear back a piece of bark. You may be distracted by the wriggle of an escaping centipede, but you will find small snails, and perhaps a shell-less slug or two. Watch the pneumostome in the slug's side open and close as it changes the air inside its mantle. The snail *Cepaea hortensis*, as big as a chestnut, is strikingly striped with brown and yellow, and a treasure to find. They are natives of Europe, brought here by Vikings or settlers, and are a favorite food of shrews because of their large size.

A Robin may turn your attention from the underlog, as he flies to a fir bough quite close,

screaming his scolding call. Then he exits with a few clucking whistles, rusty breast and white undertail flashing beneath his black back as he goes; he dodges deftly between close-standing trees and is soon out of sight.

Water from rain and melted snow is held by the rainforest as in a reservoir, and trickles into a network of small forest streams which join to form rivers of steady flow and clear water, not overflowing their banks as often as those that drain cleared land, and never drying up. Rivière de Ste. Anne, Parc de la Gaspésie, P.Q. 3 October 1977

Eastern Mixed Forest and Cleared Land

The cool, moist climate and rolling, well-drained terrain of granite, schist, limestone, shale, sandstone, and glacial till of inland areas from the Maritime provinces to the Adirondack Mountains provide good conditions for a large number of eastern tree species, both coniferous and deciduous. This habitat is not severe or restricting, so plants and animals that are generally adapted to life in a north temperate climate are widespread within it. Disturbance of the original forest by fire, logging, and agriculture has favored some of these species over others. This chapter is based both on forests and cleared land near Pugwash, Nova Scotia; Harcourt and Fredericton, New Brunswick; and North Hatley, Quebec.

The hillsides, viewed from the road, are smooth domes of variegated autumn color; red, orange, various yellows and browns, light green and dark, all intermingled. The hilltops are lighter in color where deep-rooted hardwoods, growing more vigorously in the deeper soil there, tend to exclude coniferous trees. On low land where groundwater levels are often very near the surface, plants with shallow, widely spreading roots grow well, so the valleys are clothed with the deep greens of the Balsam Fir, and Red and Black Spruce. Tamarack, which is tolerant of wet, acid conditions, grows slowly and is intolerant of shade. Although it grows best in well-drained soil, it is found most often in the open forests of damp, boggy places. In the autumn, before the Tamaracks drop their needles, they glow among the other conifers like trees of gold. White Cedar does not tolerate acid conditions, and only flourishes in a few places where moist soil overlies a calcareous bedrock.

      Long bands of alder bushes flank streams and line ditches. Their last few dull-green leaves blend with the reddish-brown twigs into a distant mysterious purple color. White Elms spread their solitary umbrella crowns high above forests in broad river valleys. When the land was settled, elms were left standing because their dense wood, springy and twisted, is difficult to saw for lumber or split for fuel. The White Pine is also a landmark tree, especially noticeable where a few individuals grow among the hardwoods on hilltops, or where one stands on a windswept hillcrest, gesturing with broad shelves of soft needles and long graceful branches. Many of these are in places where lumber was inaccessible to loggers. Others were left uncut because of multiple and contorted trunks, the effects of White Pine Weevil larvae, which hollowed out the topmost twig of each growing trunk, so that there was a wild scramble for dominance of growth among the remaining upper branches.

The autumn litter on the floor of the forest is a marvelous mixture of deciduous leaf shapes, colors, and textures. Sprinkled throughout are the dry, brown fallen leaves of nearly every kind of eastern conifer. Evergreens lend a darkness to the under-canopy world of the mixed forest, which persists even when the other trees are bare of leaves. With less light, fewer ground-covering plants are found here than in purely deciduous woods. Among them are low, shade-tolerant Herb Dogwood with four broad, parallel-veined leaves, Wintergreen with tough, round, glossy leaves, and the stiff, brown, dried stems of summer's ghostly white Indian Pipe.

Clubmosses abound. This group of primitive plants, sometimes called running pines, spreads over the ground or beneath the surface by rootstocks much like their leafy stems. Patching the rocks, mingled mosses and leafy liverworts seem to be stuffed with trapped leaf litter. Where they fail to cover the rock, a loose, pale turquoise lichen spreads in lacy circles. Lifting a flat stone may expose smooth, velvety beetle grubs, sleeping, curled like fat brown cats, on their sides. They are shorter and firmer now than when they first went to sleep, having lost some of their body water to avoid injury from frost. They begin to stir restlessly in the harsh light. Cover them back over. Under another stone is a pile of yellow birch fruits, tiny foxtails of winged seeds, strung tightly along short stems. Some rodent, perhaps a chipmunk, has secreted them here for threshing and eating when it wakes up, hungry, in the middle of winter. Few acorns are found beneath the oaks, but you may find a cache, and probably have already heard the creature to whom it belongs. After an extended chatter from a high vantage point, a Red Squirrel gallops along a fallen ash tree to disappear around the trunk of a tall, straight Jack Pine, and later, calls again from some farther part of its district.

White-throated Sparrow, *Zonotrichia albicollis*. These birds spend much of their time in the autumn on the forest floor, scratching and shuffling the leaf litter in search of seeds and insects. Campground, Parc de la Gaspésie, P.Q. 2 October 1977

A family of Gray Jays arrives. They are subtly beautiful, with gray backs, long legs softly gray-feathered to the knees, white fronts, and broadly fanned blue tails. They investigate you and assess your potential for providing food, uttering throaty squeaks, "Urk, urk," and "Piurk, piurk." Even on rainy days, although they are wet and scraggly-looking, they remain persistent at their rounds of food and territory, checking the same places in the same order, and at the same times of day. In autumn, the young look much like their parents, but they follow and beg, squatting, fluttering their wings, and dashing after food to snatch it from the adults. Gray Jays mate for life, hold the same territory for life, and stay there year round. Their wing and tail feathers are wide and silky, not narrow and stiff like those of migrating birds. Gray Jay wings are long and broad, for gliding from tree to tree, dropping from tree to ground, and rising to the next tree. Their salivary glands are specially large, for in order to survive long, cold winters in one small place, they store as much food as they can. Mixing food with sticky saliva within their crops, they then fasten lumps of the mixture to the twigs and branches of trees. In

The clubmosses or "running pines" of the eastern mixed forest. North of Fredericton, N.B. 19 October 1977. (*Lycopdium inundatum*, from Louvicourt, P.Q. May 1975)

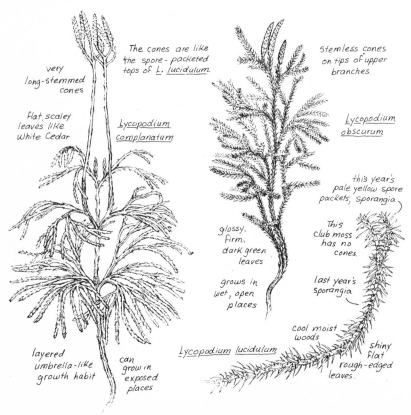

very long-stemmed cones

The cones are like the spore-packeted tops of *L. lucidulum*.

Flat, scaley leaves like White Cedar

Lycopodium complanatum

layered umbrella-like growth habit

can grow in exposed places

Stemless cones on tips of upper branches

Lycopodium obscurum

glossy, firm, dark green leaves

grows in wet, open places

Lycopodium lucidulum

this year's pale yellow spore packets, sporangia

This club moss has no cones.

last year's sporangia

cool moist woods

shiny flat rough-edged leaves.

spring, while parent birds are busy feeding nestlings instead of storing food, their salivary glands are smaller in size.

As one learns to recognize different kinds of trees, there is a distinct pleasure in the sight of them, and nearness to them. When you find them standing close together in the forest, with leaves and branches all overhead, their trunks can be as familiar, and as distinct from one another as the faces of old friends. Even in the dark, maple can be told from Ironwood, Beech from birch, and spruce from pine, by the touch of a hand.

Much of the eastern mixed forest has been logged once or many times. With modern machinery, the easiest method is to cut every tree. After the canopy is removed, many shade-tolerant mosses, ferns, and wildflowers are crowded out by other kinds, whose growth is increased tremendously by the new brightness. Birch and Beech stumps sprout clumps of new trees, and shade-intolerant herbs, shrubs, and trees invade: Fireweed, shrub dogwoods, willows, poplars, and many others.

Bracket fungi jut from the bark of dead trees, and mushrooms which grow on dead roots flourish. *Caldonia* lichens of many kinds, noticeably British Soldiers, take advantage of the abundance of light and space. Their crimson match-head fruiting tips are sometimes so abundant that the lichen mat appears to be spattered with fresh blood.

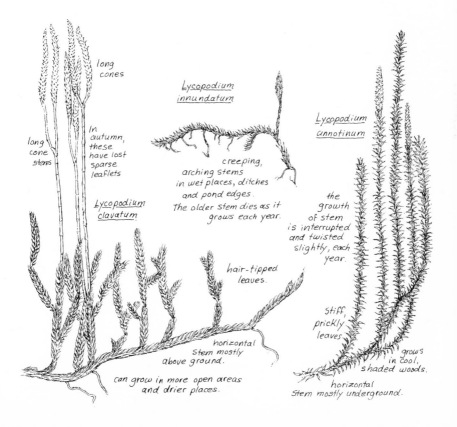

long cones

Lycopodium innundatum

Lycopodium annotinum

long cone stems

In autumn, these have lost sparse leaflets

creeping, arching stems in wet places, ditches and pond edges. The older stem dies as it grows each year.

the growth of stem is interrupted and twisted slightly, each year.

Lycopodium clavatum

hair-tipped leaves.

stiff, prickly leaves.

horizontal stem mostly above ground.

grows in cool, shaded woods.

can grow in more open areas and drier places.

horizontal stem mostly underground.

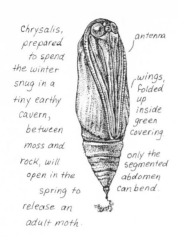

Chrysalis, prepared to spend the winter snug in a tiny earthy cavern, between moss and rock, will open in the spring to release an adult moth.

antenna

wings, folded up inside green covering

only the segmented abdomen can bend.

The lichen *Baeomyces roseus* covers exposed soil with a fine, pale green crustiness, glowing with fruiting bodies like white-stalked pink marshmallows. *Polytrichum commune*, Hair Cap Moss, named for the hairiness of the calyptra which protects its immature spore capsules, forms starry green pillows over damp acidic soil, most lush where *Sphagnum* fills the wet hollows.

Against roadside ditches, the forest grows like a hedge. Alders, Pussy Willows, Buckthorn, and Red Osier Dogwood fill the space below the tree crowns. The ground is covered with Bracken, Ostrich Fern, and Sweetfern, which isn't a fern, but a branching, woody-stemmed bush, its wavy edged, fernlike leaves aromatic with a pungent, spicy sweetness.

A tree frog, *Hyla crucifer* "peeps" plaintively from a waterfilled part of a grassy ditch, an autumn reminder of coming spring activities. After the long months of winter, ponds and ditches will be filled with water from melting snow, and roiling with mating Spotted and Blue-spotted Salamanders. The air will shrill with the calls of tree frogs and reverberate with the voices of Wood Frogs and Leopard Frogs, while from the woods will sound the deep halting hoots of the Great Horned Owl, and the harsh metallic whistle of the tiny Saw Whet Owl.

Open wasteland, gouged with ponds and ditches reminds some people only of the loss of the original forest; but for many reptiles and amphibians, rodents, rabbits, foxes, deer, and birds, the shrubby, sunlit stages of early succession after disturbance offers much better opportunity for feeding and reproduction than does second growth or climax forest.

In cleared land that is grazed by livestock, fast-growing plants, such as chickweed, plantain, Heal-all, speedwell, Yarrow, and White Clover flourish, tolerant of trampling and grazing. Grasses with low, broad leaves and bent stems can stand having their tops cropped often,

The House Cricket, *Acheta domestica*, came to North America from Europe with early settlers. It lives in and near farm buildings. Bishops Mills, S of Kemptville, Ont. 22 October 1977

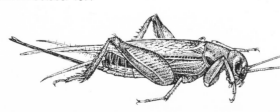

and if they don't have time to bear seed, they reproduce vegetatively by underground rhizomes, and maintain a dense, rain-absorbent ground cover. Dandelions adapt to closely grazed pastures. They escape being eaten by having their splayed leaves pressed flat against the grass and by bearing short-stemmed flowers. The most noticeable pasture plants are those that grow to their full height undisturbed by livestock; spiny thistles, bitter milkweed, prickle-haired Blueweed, resiny common Juniper, wooly-leaved Mullein, and coarse-stemmed goldenrod.

In the middle of a heavily grazed field, a rock pile can be a wild place. Broken twigs and stems of trampled plants lodge in drifts about its margins and small fronds of Hayscented Fern peek from between boulders. Here a gangly harvestman, or "Daddy Longlegs" poises, not a spider at all, but more closely related to mites. A big, brown true spider crouches, discovered, where she has made a silk nest for herself in the crack between two slabs of stone; and as you look inside, a sowbug, like a tiny tailless armadillo, quickly makes itself scarce.

Cow droppings are special places too. I have flipped dry crusty pats of dung, and found them riddled with tunnels made by the dung beetles *Aphodius*, North American relatives of sacred Egyptian scarabs. When they folded their legs to play dead, they looked and felt like red and black ceramic beads. There were glossy, dark brown earwigs there too, with curved, shining pincers at the ends of their abdomens.

The edge of the forest slowly reclaims abandoned pastures, or those lightly grazed, as cedars venture past the fences, and aspen and birch saplings begin where the goldenrod, Salsify, and Yarrow are untrampled. In the light shade of the tall weeds, perfectly formed little spruces grow, flexible trunks still tightly needled. The grasses grow taller and narrow leaved. They are parted by mosses and lichens here and there. Sapling maples raise long straight branchlets above you, a few broad yellow leaves atop each one. Black-capped Chickadees have formed their winter feeding flocks, and flit about like air-borne mice from twig to twig through the cedars and birches, always very busy but curious. They approach much more closely than other birds would, to see what you are, and why you sit so still on the grass. Nearer and nearer they venture, until you can see the breaths they take, and all the quick movements of their lively, feathered bodies.

The Meadow Vole,
Microtus pennsylvanicus

Eastern Deciduous Forest

The region of deciduous forest in North America lies mostly in the eastern United States, and extends into southern Ontario. Some of the more southern species of hardwood, such as the Tulip Tree, Black Gum, Sycamore, Sassafrass, and Pawpaw, extend their range to the north shore of Lake Erie. The land is mostly well-drained glacial till, overlying old deposits of limestone and shale, and favors the deep-rooting hardwoods. The most common of these are the cold-tolerant species of maple, Beech, oak, and Basswood. This chapter is based mainly on Mark S. Burnham Provincial Park, near Peterborough, 18.5 km northwest of Douglas, Renfrew County, Point Pelee National Park, and woods near Guelph, in Ontario.

The wind blows freely across fields and roads, hissing over the drifting snow. The very same wind moves through the branches at the top of the forest with a hushing roar. Below, in the sanctuary of the trees, the vapor of your breath floats almost motionless, and the sound of the wind's rage comes to you softly, muffled like the ocean's echo in a seashell. The forest doesn't seem empty, just quiet. In January the snow is deep on the forest floor, and travel here without skis or snowshoes is nearly impossible.

All winter, the leafless trees stand gaunt and gray, like the framework of an unfinished building. Snow dominates the landscape, undulating over stumps and logs, and balancing heavily on the flat, dark-needled boughs of occasional Hemlocks. Faded tissue-thin Beech leaves, like ghosts of sunlight, still attached to the twigs of lower branches whisper faintly to a gentle puff of freezing air.

The thin layer of living wood fiber under the bark of hardwoods cannot withstand temperatures below minus forty degrees without being severely damaged. In order to survive any temperature below freezing, they lose much of their moisture in autumn. The well-known rising of the sap in spring is the replacement of this moisture, enriched with sugar and minerals from the roots, so that leaves and flowers can grow. The northern hardwoods, Beech, Sugar Maple, Yellow Birch, Red Oak, and Basswood, all have their northern limits about where the winter temperatures reach forty degrees below zero and there are replaced by conifers, aspen, and Paper Birch.

Without their foliage, the forest trees look much alike at first glance, but noticing trunk shapes, bark textures, branching patterns, and the character and arrangement of winter buds, makes one realize that they are really all quite different. Sugar Maple, Beech, Basswood, Red Oak, Yellow Birch, Red Maple, White Ash, and White Oak are the tree species most often encountered here, and after you have become acquainted with them, the less common trees are exciting to discover.

Some southern trees have been found naturally occurring in only a few places north of the southern Great Lakes, but Ironwood is one of the more common. Its slender trunk is clothed by a gray-brown bark of

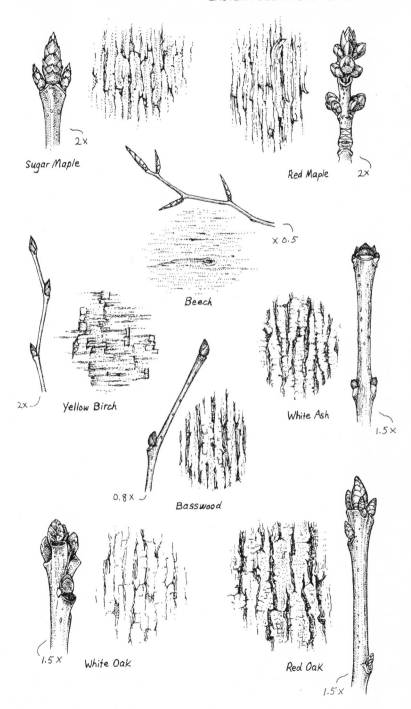

Sugar Maple   2×

Red Maple   2×

× 0.5

Beech

Yellow Birch   2×

White Ash

1.5 ×

0.8 ×   Basswood

White Oak   1.5 ×

Red Oak   1.5 ×

long, narrow, broken strips, which
shrink to spring out at their ends,
and its long branches arch upward
with thin, dark reddish twigs and
pointed, green-brown buds. Black
Cherry has dark bark with
rectangular scales, sometimes still
bearing the pale, horizontal
lenticel marks so prominent on its
smooth, reddish-brown younger
bark. The bark of the Shagbark
Hickory is distinctively fractured
and curled in loose, ragged strips
lifting outward from the trunk. The
Butternut's gray trunk is deeply
grooved, with diamond-shaped
patterns of flat ridges, and its
lateral buds are bunched along
the sides of stout, pale brown
twigs. Hackberry's shape is like
that of an elm, and the crisp ridges
of its untidy gray-brown bark are
curled like broken blisters. Its
greenish twigs are finely fuzzy,
with closely spaced, alternate
buds. The uncommon Black Gum
tree may be recognized by the
way in which its dark gray, thickly ridged bark is broken into irregular
bands of short segments. The Tulip Tree, also a southern species, is
found in Canada only in southernmost Ontario along Lakes Ontario and
Erie. Its ruler-straight brown trunk is barked with long, closely spaced,
rounded ridges, and its stout twigs are encircled by a line at each leaf
scar.

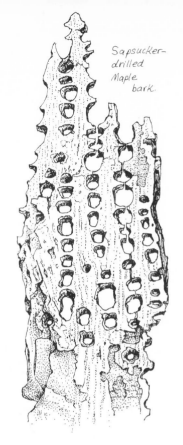

Sapsucker-
drilled
Maple
bark.

   The Eastern Hemlock is the only evergreen conifer characteristic
of the eastern deciduous forest. Like the Western Hemlock it is very
shade-tolerant, and so can grow with mature hardwoods on rich, moist
soil. Its dark green leaves make enough food in dim light so that it
needn't shoot a long, naked trunk up toward the canopy to compete with

grouse droppings
found in winter

actual size

other trees for light. Notice how its lower branches touch the snow, and look there for evidence of grouse or rabbit refuge.

The soft snow blanket reflects no sound but, instead, records all things that touch its surface. Many impressions on the smooth white surface may be made by clumps of snow, blown from branches, but there are others, too. Even on the coldest days, when warm-blooded life stays safe under the snow of the fields, here in the stillness of the forest it runs about on the surface. A series of small heart-shaped depressions and tail marks show where a White-footed Mouse hopped in soft snow. Rabbits leave two prints of petite forepaws, one after the other, alternating with prints of long oval hind feet, side by side. Where the rabbit tracks circle raspberry, Hobblebush, and young birch, you can see where buds and twigs were snipped off by straight-edged incisors. Rabbits and hares don't store food. This hedge clipping is their only means of winter sustenance. In years of high rabbit population, bushes and young trees are cut back to the snow line.

Gray Squirrel tracks resemble those of young rabbits because of their long hind feet, but their movements usually can be traced to the bases of trees where their winter nests or drays can sometimes be seen: big balls of leaves and twigs in the forks of high branches. I have found holes dug straight down through the snow, showing bits of disturbed leaf litter and black earth within, and wondered if some squirrel had found here its treasure, buried before snowfall, long months ago.

A weasel has been tunneling just under the surface of the snow. The straight line of its collapsed passage runs for a meter or two, and then there is a hole where it sat up to take its bearings before continuing for a short distance in a slightly different direction. Perhaps it was searching for the scent of shrews or mice. Some of the smallest of

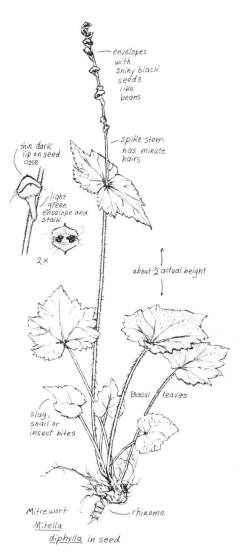

envelopes with shiny black seeds like beans

spike stem has minute hairs

thin dark lip on seed case

light green envelope and stalk

2×

about ½ actual height

Basal leaves

slug, snail or insect bites

Mitrewort
Mitella
diphylla in seed

— rhizome

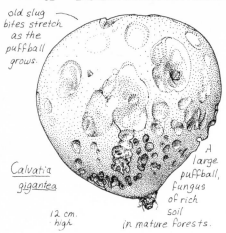

old slug bites stretch as the puffball grows.

Calvatia gigantea

12 cm. high

A large puffball, fungus of rich soil in mature forests.

tracks are left by the tiny naked feet of *Blarina*, the Short-tailed Shrew, which is very active, even in winter, since it still must eat about half its own body weight in food each day. On firm snow, even the minute marks of its delicate toes can be seen. Now the shrew may be back in its nest, licking warmth back into those cold toes. In low temperatures, the exposed tail, feet, nose, and ears of any animal will become very cold as the blood vessels constrict to avoid losing too much body heat through extremities. It is better to lose the tip of an ear or tail by frostbite than to supply cold blood to vital internal organs.

You will not find the tracks of the long-tailed Woodland Jumping Mouse in the winter snow, for this little mammal, like the bat and the Groundhog, is a true hibernator. Its body cools, and its breathing and heartbeat slow in the autumn, very much like those of cold-blooded animals. You may find a hibernating jumping mouse sometime, curled in a nest of leaves in a hollow stump or between the roots of a tree, before the snow comes to bury it. It lies peaceful and still, and there are long pauses between breaths. Waking up from complete hibernation takes nearly an hour, while the blood vessels around the heart and brain open wider and the heartbeat quickens, rousing the animal, front end first.

Other mammals that sleep in winter do so less deeply. Their body temperatures drop only a little below normal, and every week or so, they wake for a breath of fresh air and perhaps some food. When the winter weather warms a little, Raccoons wake and climb from their hollow trees to forage for torpid frogs and sluggish crayfish where stream banks are ice-free. Skunks are also light sleepers with nocturnal habits, and emerge from hollow logs to dig wherever they can for motionless snails, snakes, and even sleeping jumping mice or chipmunks. The chipmunk stays in its burrow for most of the winter, waking often to eat from its stores of seeds and nuts and to warm its body when the temperature drops too low. Its body is not insulated by a thick layer of fat as most other mammals are in winter; but like all hibernators, it has a special deposit of dense brown fat between its shoulder blades which is rich in protein and in iron-containing respiratory pigments which help to warm its body while it awakens.

An irregular tapping sound in the top of a big gray-barked maple is the hammering of a Hairy Woodpecker on a dead branch. Most of the kinds of birds that you will see in the winter forest are hunting, in one way or another, for insects wintering in the trees. The Hairy Woodpecker chops holes through bark in search of wood-boring beetle larvae, and the smaller Downy Woodpecker gleans branchlets for insect pupae and eggs, while flocks of chickadees inspect the twigs.

Nearly invisible against the bark, with almost inaudible high-pitched cries, Brown Creepers spiral up tree trunks searching the crevices in rough bark, for eggs and sleeping insects. White-breasted Nuthatches comment, "Ank, ank,"

The Five-lined Skink, *Eumeces fasciatus*, lives around damp, rotting logs and eats insects. Point Pelee, Ont.

in soft nasal voices, roving like blue-gray shadows all over the trunks, as if there really were no right side up, or upside down, and the whole world were tree bark.

Large flocks of crossbills and grosbeaks are nomadic in wintertime, clustering raucously in the seed-laden crowns of ash and Hemlock, stripping them bare and then moving on. Heavy-bodied Ruffed Grouse, and thick-billed, bright-plumaged Pine and Evening Grosbeaks prefer the high protein content of seeds, but often must stuff their crops with buds when seeds cannot be found. Thus they ensure their survival until spring on what the trees had stored for next year's leaf production.

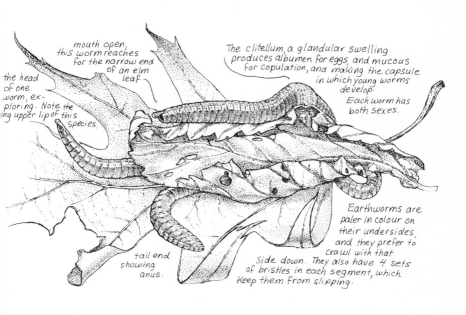

mouth open, this worm reaches for the narrow end of an elm leaf

the head of one worm, exploring. Note the ng upper lip of this species.

The clitellum, a glandular swelling produces albumen for eggs, and mucous for copulation, and making the capsule in which young worms develop. Each worm has both sexes.

tail end showing anus.

Earthworms are paler in colour on their undersides, and they prefer to crawl with that side down. They also have 4 sets of bristles in each segment, which keep them from slipping.

Great Lakes Harbor

The Great Lakes are the largest area of fresh water in the world, remnants of huge landlocked glacial lakes. Their fish and bird life is more like that of the sea than of smaller inland lakes. This chapter is based mostly on observations at Toronto, Ontario.

In winter, freshwater harbors are locked in ice. Beyond the quays and breakwaters, the water is roughened by winds and disturbed by storms. All winter there is a contest between ice and open water. Ice extends out over the surface in calm, cold weather, and is heaved up, broken, and piled against the shore in rough weather. The ice coatings on rocks and on the long straight lines of concrete breakwaters are thick, and elaborately sculpted by moving water and cold. Smooth, fantastic shelves, nobs, and rippling columns of ice are lapped about by choppy dark water in which round-headed, black and white Bufflehead ducks bob, and long-tailed Oldsquaws dive, searching for food on the bottom.

Where the harbor ice has weakened and sagged, shallow pools of water glaze its surface. Here ducks and geese prefer to drink. They rest their bills on the ice so that their heads are nearly level at the ends of their arched necks, and they sip-sip-sip the cold water into their throats. Raising their heads slightly above body level, they let the water trickle down inside, and then bow to sip again.

Mallards, Black Ducks, and Canada Geese take advantage of the shelter between wharves on windy days, and here people feed and watch them. One by one, the ducks take turns drinking at water melted by the dark hull of an icebound yacht. As the sun shines some sit, some stand, and some walk quietly about on the smooth ice in the sun. Sometimes they stand on one foot, stretching the other leg back, and spreading webbed toes to be warmed by the sun.

When watching a duck preen its plumage, notice the quick rubbing motion of its bill in the feathers at the base of its tail where, protruding and covered by thin skin, there is a gland which supplies oil for waterproofing feathers. A Mallard flies in to land. It touches with feet forward, and bumps down on its breast. Tucking its feet neatly up inside its warm, dry feathers, it rests comfortably, insulated from the frozen surface. A brown-feathered Black Duck moves slowly on the dock, scooping its bill along the bottom of a shallow muddy puddle, perhaps collecting grit to grind the food in its gizzard.

Black Ducks and Mallards hybridize, sometimes with each other, and sometimes with the large domestic Mallards. This almost always scrambles color patterns, causing the white ring between the iridescent green neck and rusty bib of Mallard plumage to broaden or disappear. Hybrids with the basically dark plumage of Black Ducks often have dark green neck and head, or a broad white neckband, or a triangle of white on the breast. One of the ducks walks with a bad limp. Another seems to have throat trouble, scratching repeatedly at the base of its jaw, and opening and closing its mouth. Most Canada Geese, Mallards, and Black Ducks winter farther south where the climate is milder and food more plentiful, but the ones that are here in winter are either residents who have chosen not to risk migration, or cripples, unable to continue southward because of wounds or sickness.

When the ice and snow have melted the harbor shore is littered with all manner of things, both natural and man-made. Bleach bottles, rounded chunks of styrofoam, suntan lotion bottles, peach pits, steak bones, boards, and fishing net floats catch the eye. Less noticeable is the natural beach wash: jumbled drifts of water plants, millions of fragile snail shells sorted into bands by the waves, pale pink and ivory crayfish parts, pearly clam shells, gull feathers, bird bones, and an occasional light, dry carcass. In spring and early summer, Alewives, spent from spawning, are killed by temperature differences in the lake, and drift ashore in multitudes like silvery autumn leaves. Full of fish, the gulls sit satisfied on whitewashed rocks.

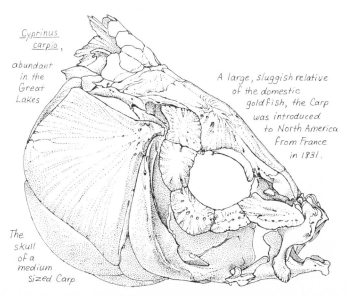

Cyprinus carpio, abundant in the Great Lakes

A large, sluggish relative of the domestic goldfish, the Carp was introduced to North America from France in 1831.

The skull of a medium sized Carp

City

The city habitat is created and dominated by people. Its main physical features are man-made, and most of its plants are cultivated. The plants and animals which live in cities are a mixture of native species and introductions, deliberate and accidental. Those which are unplanned and unbidden by man are touches of wildness within the city. This chapter is based mainly on Toronto, Ontario; and Quebec City, Quebec.

While people attend to their various concerns inside the big city buildings, birds contest for territories, nest, and raise their young, at home against the outer surfaces of those same buildings. There they find shade in summer, warmth and protection from wind in winter, and a high refuge from the noisy rushing activity of the streets and sidewalks.

Pigeons impress each other by dancing solemnly in circles, this way and that on building ledges, with tails fanned, heads bobbing, and iridescent feathers quivering on inflated necks. A throaty burbling "coo" sounds persistently above the cacophony of mingled traffic noises.

Fat brown House Sparrows swarm in a flock on the pavement, pecking busily at seeds and grit, and picking up popcorn, chips, and crumbs where people drop them. They were introduced from Europe in the 1850s, and since then have evolved adaptations to North American climates, so that House Sparrows from the southern United States are much smaller, and don't use their food as rapidly to keep warm as those in the north.

The melodious twitters and long sliding whistles of a flock of European Starlings liven the still winter air of a residential street, as they feast on the buds of a Silver Maple. Starling plumage looks plain and dark from a distance, but its purple and green iridescence is shot with tiny arrowheads of cream, and is a delight to be seen at close range.

Buildings provide specialized nest sites for two insect-eating migratory birds. Nesting only inside chimneys, Chimney Swifts have no competition for breeding sites from other species. Nighthawks nest on flat roofs, their natural preference being gravelly open places. The sound of them is an integral part of warm summer nights in the city. As traffic noise quiets a little at dusk, the "Bijjjew" calls of high, flycatching Nighthawks and the soft booms they make swooping sharply up from display dives can be heard with the twittering of the circling swifts. Bright lights compensate for the low density of insects in the city, by letting Nighthawks hunt all through the night, instead of only at dusk and dawn.

Backyard bird feeders increase the number of birds that are resident in urban areas in winter. Over time, they may even cause change in the ranges of birds. Food supplied by people in winter has helped the Evening Grosbeak to spread eastward from the Rocky Mountains and the western boreal forest, and the Cardinal and Mockingbird to spread northward into Ontario and Quebec.

Skunks and Raccoons are well known in cities as garbage thieves with truculent personalities.

Squirrels enjoy a rare position of favor among city wildlife because their boldness and small size appeals to people, and those in parks are tame and well fed. You can spend hours in city parks, watching squirrels forage for buds, seeds, tree flowers, or handouts. They chase each other about trunks and branches, leap wildly between trees from springy branchtips to springy branchtips, and carry bunches of leaves to their winter nests, or drays, high in the trees.

Perhaps the most interesting wild things in the city

House Mouse, *Mus musculus*. Introduced from Europe by early settlers, it has lived in buildings throughout recorded history. Toronto, Ont. 13 November 1973

Foreign Trees in The City

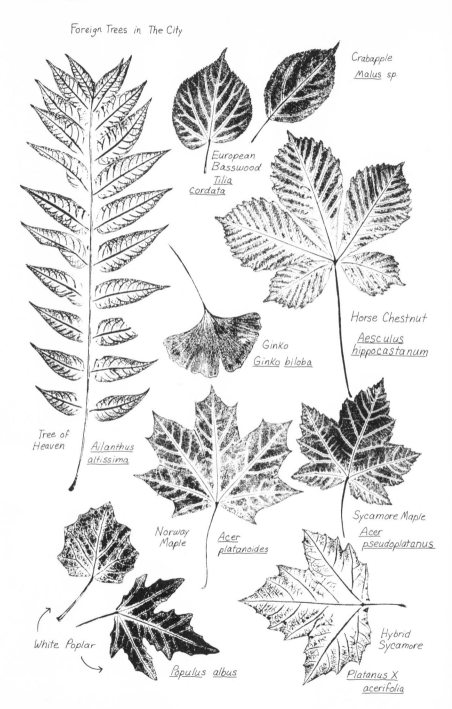

Crabapple
Malus sp.

European
Basswood
Tilia
cordata

Horse Chestnut
Aesculus
hippocastanum

Ginko
Ginko biloba

Tree of
Heaven   _Ailanthus_
altissima

Sycamore Maple
Acer
pseudoplatanus

Norway
Maple   _Acer_
platanoides

White Poplar

Populus albus

Hybrid
Sycamore

Platanus X
acerifolia

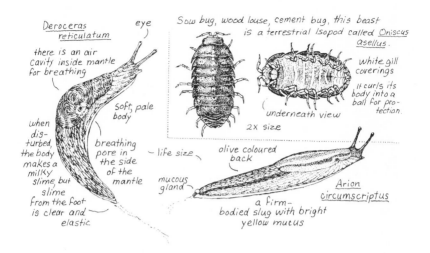

Deroceras
reticulatum

eye

there is an air
cavity inside mantle
for breathing

Sow bug, wood louse, cement bug, this beast
is a terrestrial Isopod called *Oniscus*
asellus.

white gill
coverings

It curls its
body into a
ball for pro-
tection.

soft, pale
body

underneath view
2× size

when
dis-
turbed,
the body
makes a
milky
slime, but
slime
from the foot
is clear and
elastic

breathing
pore in
the side
of the
mantle

~ life size ~

mucous
gland

olive coloured
back

Arion
circumscriptus

a firm-
bodied slug with bright
yellow mucus

are those which are unaware of people, and overlooked by people. Small snails with glistening shells inhabit some of the cracks between slabs of sidewalk and against cement walls and foundations, where they feed on algae, low mosses, and the tender shoots of small grasses. Microscopic mites live there too, and tiny gray springtails, brittle brown millipedes, and sowbugs, flat terrestrial crustaceans sometimes called cement bugs. All of these eat very small amounts of dead vegetable matter, and their bodies after death feed each other and fertilize their microhabitat of pavement crack. More mobile and heat-tolerant, small brown ants traverse the broad, sunny stretches of pavement as they forage for anything edible, following the scent trails of those who have found food.

Lawn grass harbors an intricate continuum of comings and goings, easily observed from a prone position with the aid of a hand lens. Leaf hoppers, beetles, tiny moths, spiders, and snails can be seen there by day; and by flashlight, if you are quiet and step carefully, you can watch earthworms feeding and mating in the grass on dewy nights.

A dense, pure mat of lawn grass can only survive where there is plenty of nutrient, moisture, and light. Elsewhere, mowing opens up space, and provides light for the incursion of many small, low, hardy plant species such as Dandelions, chickweed, clovers, and mosses. Everywhere you look about the city there are small undisturbed sites such as the soil around the bases of trees and telephone poles, and along driveways and fences where wild plants grow: plantain, avens, Lynchis, Deptford Pink, Herb Robert, Fleabane, speedwells, buttercups, and several species of mustards. Many of these weeds are wild relatives of showy cultivated flowers, such as *Aster, Portulaca, Geranium, Chrysanthemum*, and morning glory.

Railroad Embankment

*This chapter is based on railroad embankments in Pasadena, Newfoundland;
Canaan Station, New Brunswick; Ottawa and Guelph, Ontario; Waboden and
Churchill, Manitoba; Salmo and Qualicum Beach, British Columbia.*

Through city and countryside, the railroad right-of-way is protected from
cultivation and development. Looking out of a train window, one doesn't
notice the familiar narrow strip of railroad habitat, just the changing
landscape beyond. On foot, as you step from tie to tie, or walk with
crunching steps on the gravel, the tracks stretch monotonously on
before you.

Plants that grow here are a mixture of the characteristic species of
each area and widespread weeds of dry soil. In wooded areas,
Raspberry, alder bushes, and Red Osier Dogwood may line a fence or
forest edge, and cattails and sedges rise from waterfilled ditches.
Conditions are most rigorous in the porous gravel of the embankment,
where moisture is scarce, even after rain. Dandelions splay flat rosettes
of jagged green leaves over rough gravel among a few straggly wisps
of yellow grass beside the tracks. Adventurous, pioneering strawberries
advance runners from the edge of grassy patches. You will find these
thin runners marked with meagre bunches of tooth-edged red leaves

wherever they can root among the stones. Bright green patches of soft, bottlebrush Field Horsetail, *Equisetum arvense* spread through the gravel by underground runners, and slowly accumulate a moisture-retaining bed for themselves of each year's hollow gray skeletons of stems and thin branches.

Thrifty Burdock, plantain, Teasel, and Mullein spread broad leaves on the ground in their first year of growth. In the next year, they raise tall woody stems bearing flowers high, so that the wind or passing animals may disperse their seed. Strong, deep tap roots anchor the lofty flower stalks and reach far down for water. Their low flat leaves keep other plants from growing close and competing for moisture. An embankment may be completely clothed with Bracken fern, once a sea of waving fronds, and now richly rust-colored and curling to crispness in the autumn sun. Goldenrod, competing fiercely with grasses, may blanket large areas with frothy yellow bloom, supported by hard, straight, hairy-leaved stems. In the prairies, some railroad right-of-ways are refuges for native grasses that once covered the tallgrass prairie.

Weed and grass seeds have ways of getting stuck in all kinds of places, and when they invade a new area, they often occur first along railways. They may be carried by cars, people, or cargo from one railway yard or siding to another. Those well suited to grow on dry open soil may easily become established anywhere they fall along the line. Both plants and animals can disperse along the continuous habitat of the railroad embankment, built up high and dry, even through swamps, muskeg, and rugged terrain.

The gravel of the roadbed is often at least partly composed of limestone, which is easy to quarry and crush. Snails can always be found near limestone, because it provides calcium for their shells. Small species such as glossy, long-shelled *Cionella*, and flat, finely ribbed *Vallonia* are frequently found among grass roots and under rain-sodden scraps of litter. Large, bright yellow and brown-banded *Cepaea* snails often climb up onto dry surfaces to sleep, fastening themselves with a thin parchment-like membrane. Their moist bodies are pulled back inside and may survive long periods of cold or drought. This conspicuous European snail has spread its range so readily along the railway that it is tempting to think that snails may be carried by trains as well as plant seeds are, along the homogeneous stretch of habitat that is the railroad embankment.

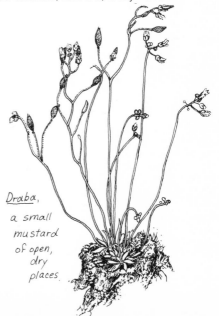

Draba,
a small
mustard
of open,
dry
places

Limestone

Limestone is rock made of calcium carbonate. It forms by precipitation or the accumulation of fossil shells in layers on the ocean bottom. It often occurs with dolomite, which is harder and rich in magnesium as well as calcium, and shale, which is compacted clay. Under heat and pressure within the earth, limestone becomes marble, which has the same chemical properties, but doesn't erode as easily. These calcium-rich bedrocks are most often noticed where erosion of the soft, red, green, and black shale has exposed cliffs and banks of hard, pale stone, and where glaciers have scraped it clear of overlying material leaving large, flat tables of rock. This chapter is based mostly on observations made on the Niagara Escarpment, on the Bruce Peninsula, at Rockwood and Campbellville, and near Kingston, Ontario; in Gatineau County, Quebec; along Manitoba Highway 6; and near Inuvik, Northwest Territories.

You can see the creamy irregular face of the limestone escarpment above its forested lower slopes as you hike toward it over pasture fields. The effect of the limestone is rich, even though the escarpment itself cannot be farmed. Soil made of humus and eroded limestone is an excellent foundation for plant and animal life. Near the base of the escarpment the ground is rocky with pieces of limestone, called talus, broken from the cliffs.

Limestone talus is favored by cold-blooded vertebrates. Wood Frogs, tree frogs, salamanders, and snakes avoid freezing during the winter by crawling below the frost line through the dark, damp maze of spaces between jumbled talus rock. Rattlesnakes are not often found, even if you are looking for them, but it is wise, when turning ground cover in regions where these poisonous snakes live, to lift the edge that faces away from you, so that if there happens to be a rattlesnake resting there, it won't see you before you see it.

On rocky slopes farming is difficult, so the forest remains. It has tied the deep jumble of broken rock together with tree roots, and covered it with rich black humus. Sugar Maple, elm, Basswood, and White Ash are characteristic of mineral-rich, low-acid soils, and bathe the slope in cool moist shadow. Earthworms thrive in limy soil and, hardly do the leaves fall from the trees, but earthworms drag them into their burrows

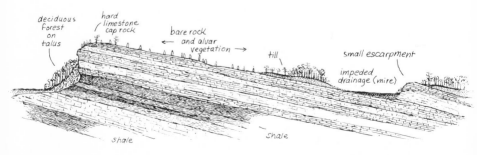

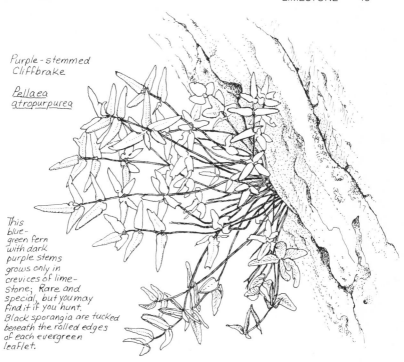

Purple-stemmed
Cliffbrake.

Pellaea
atropurpurea

This
blue-
green fern
with dark
purple stems
grows only in
crevices of lime-
stone; Rare and
special, but you may
find it if you hunt.
Black sporangia are tucked
beneath the rolled edges
of each evergreen
leaflet.

and digest them into fine black loam. Snails are abundant wherever there is limestone and, if you look closely, you will find many kinds. *Anguispira* is most common. Its finely ribbed shell is marked with a brown herringbone pattern. *Triodopsis* has a heavy, large and nutlike shell with a thick white rim. Round glossy zonitids, *Cionella* with long, amber, many-whorled shells, and *Succinea*, are more versatile snails, with thinner shells that need less calcium than *Anguispira* and *Triodopsis*.

Bold efts, the terrestrial young of the pond dwelling newt, march

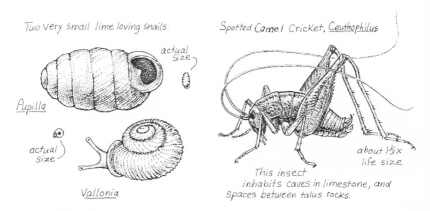

Two very small lime loving snails.

actual
size

Pupilla

actual
size

Vallonia

Spotted Camel Cricket, *Ceuthophilus*

about 1⅓x
life size

This insect
inhabits caves in limestone, and
spaces between talus rocks.

Rose Pogonia or Snake-mouth

Orchid

Pogonia ophenglossoides

Butterwort

Flowers shaped like those of its relative, the water plant, Bladder-wort

Pinguicula vulgaris

about the forest floor in damp weather. They have no fear of being eaten because their rough scarlet skin is deadly poisonous. Red Efts and Blue-spotted and Red-backed Salamanders hide beneath the flat stones of the talus. Turning stones along the banks of streams may expose a quick flicker of a slippery, golden-brown Two-lined Salamander.

The small, dark, smooth-scaled Ring-necked Snake, named for its golden neckband, hides under stones and in rotting wood, and feeds mostly on earthworms and small salamanders.

As the slope becomes steeper, you may find it easier to pick your way from rock to rock up the stream bed, while the water runs past you down through the forest on an obstacle course of flat shelves, pools, and tumbled stones. Many *Physa* snails are even crawling on wet rocks above the surface of the stream, out of the constant current of the cold, rushing water, and stonefly nymphs come a little out of the water to munch on semiaquatic moss. Many of the stones bear imprints and fossilized remains of coral and shells, imbedded long ago when the stone was soft

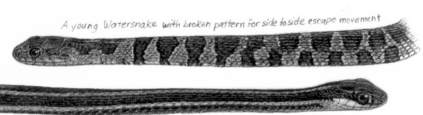

A young Watersnake with broken pattern for side to side escape movement

A young Ribbon Snake, striped for forward movement through grass.

sediment on the bottom of a tropical sea. Suddenly, boulders block your way where the stream, with a hollow echo in its voice, bursts from a dark underground waterway fed by seepage through the limestone above.

Leaving the noise of the stream behind, you find yourself avoiding slippery moss and crumbling shale, and grasping trees for support as you go up the steep rocky slope. The trees also clutch for support, reaching strong roots around edges and over rock faces, like grotesquely exaggerated human fingers, searching for cracks and fissures and filling them as they grow. They pry apart as many rocks as they help to anchor. The landscape is vertical. Some surfaces are rough and chalky, supporting only a few scraps of lichen; and some, damp and sheltered, are upholstered with moss, embroidered with liverworts, and planted with many kinds of ferns which sprout from crevices like green fountains.

In the east, long, narrow fronds of Bulblet Fern are nearly always found where there is limestone. Besides the usual method of sexual reproduction by spores, this fern grows round green bulblets about the size of match heads. These drop from the undersides of the leaves and germinate asexually into new plants. Here you may also see a strange little plant whose narrow, pointed, arching leaves grow younger plants of its kind wherever they have touched their tips to the moss. This is the Walking Fern, found only in damp, shady limestone places.

The Common Polypody fern crowns shaded rocks and ledges in leathery green profusion. It and Maidenhair Fern, Slender Cliffbrake, Maidenhair Spleenwort, and *Woodsia* ferns all grow in moist shaded cracks and crevices of calcareous rocks. The polypody has close relatives in the west, and the other species of fern are found in limestone areas both east of the prairies and in the western mountains.

Trillium, Wild Ginger, Helleborine Orchid, and Miterwort are noticeable wildflowers of forested talus slopes. Wild Columbine coyly nods its scarlet flower there too, as well as on more exposed places on the top of the escarpment.

Near the brink of the cliff the canopy opens, exposing rock faces to erosion. The softer layers of stone are carved away, and the surface is sculpted into long horizontal bands by wind and rain. In gullies and ravines on either side of barren, jutting rock faces, Red Cedar, *Juniperus virginiana*, with scaled leaves and misty blue fleshy cones that look like berries, grows upright, with dense, prickly foliage and springy branches. Pushing past them and around and over mammoth chunks of limestone that have fractured from the hard cap rock is laborious work. But you may be rewarded by discoveries of long crevices resplendent with Purple-stemmed Cliffbrake or dense, woolly stands of *Woodsia* fronds. Delicate evergreen Wall Rue springs undaunted from thin cracks, reviving with each rain, after seeming withered and dead. On wide ledges, and above on the escarpment, in cracks too small to hold enough soil for Red Cedar, Common Juniper sprawls fragrant prickly branches, growing individually, and in springy mats of continuous ground cover.

The slightly sloping crest of the escarpment is dominated by narrow Red Cedars and the occasional splendid White Pine, with long, sky-sweeping boughs. Glaciers have bared much of the bedrock of the limestone regions, and left, here and there, surface deposits of sand and gravel. These allow better drainage, some access to groundwater, and a tolerable balance of acid and calcium for a wide variety of plants. Conditions are rigorous for plants where there is no surface drainage — in alvars, which are seasonally wet, and in mires, which are continually wet.

On patches of bare rock, crusts of lichen and cushions of short, drought-tolerant mosses slowly dissolve the rock beneath them, building a little soil. Where water collects in shallow, temporary pools in the spring, the only plants that can tolerate both spring flood and summer drought are an alga, a liverwort, and a short, yellowish moss. These grow on a thin layer of soil, washed from the roots of nearby vegetation. A dark band of short, dense mosses surrounds these special plants. Sometimes a small succulent, *Portulaca oleracea*, with thick, paddle-shaped leaves, and tiny yellow flowers grows in this mat. Panic Grass and fine, tufted Hair Grass border it with a paler zone, in which are also found willow-herb, Hedge Hyssop, and False Pennyroyal: flowering plants which can grow in thin and limy soils. Bluish-green Wire Grass and a tall, coarse sedge grow beyond, in deeper soil, sometimes with Sicklepod, a mustard with long, drooping seed pods. This strict arrangement of vegetation in seasonally wet areas of shallow soil makes a beautiful mosaic-like pattern of plant color, tone, and texture.

Some water seeps down slopes through the vegetation, trickling over exposed rock. Some soaks slowly through the limestone bedrock to the level of the groundwater, or water table, where the rock is saturated. Depressions in the bedrock, where the water table is at the surface much of the year, are called mires. These accumulate a wet layer of sandy clay from broken-down limestone, and organic material from plant decomposition. During dry times, the groundwater, containing calcium carbonate dissolved from the limestone, moves upward, evaporating from the surface of the mire, and leaving a deposit of calcium carbonate called marl. Phosphorus, an essential mineral, dissolves so slowly in such calcareous conditions that rapid plant growth is impossible, and the plants that live in mires must also tolerate levels of calcium that would poison other species. Pitcher Plants and sundews can live in both acid and limy habitats. These plants specialize in eating insects to supplement the minerals that the soil cannot supply. Butterwort, rolling its greasy yellowish leaves around insects, is a carnivorous plant that prefers mires to bogs. Like the desert, bog, tundra, and exposed bedrock, the mire is an open, sunny place, with plenty of light for the plants which live there. These habitats, in their own ways, are very restricting to life, and plants which can overcome the hardships that exclude most others, are privileged with easy availability of some resources.

Limestone bedrock also lies beneath part of the boreal forest. In Manitoba, the "Interlake" area, between Lakes Manitoba and Winnipeg is a vast plain of glacial till on flat limestone. It floods in spring, and is very dry during the summer. Hay and cattle are raised in the south, and the north is forested with Jack Pine and spruce.

In the fall, thousands of garter snakes gather, their black bodies brilliantly yellow-striped and red-spotted. They hibernate in sinkholes, places where limestone has collapsed into caves dissolved beneath the surface. The males remain at the sinkholes for most of the spring, and in writhing masses compete to mate with the emerging females.

Even as far north as the lower Mackenzie Valley, almost at the tree line, limestone bedrock favors shelled animals. Willow bushes and patches of sedge grow on clean gray dolomite around a sinkhole lake, and tiny snails are abundant in the twisted brown leaves beneath the willows. Here, where summer is brief, they grow slowly, perhaps active for only a few weeks each year. Empty whitened shells accumulate over the decades, protected from corrosive organic acids by cold and by the lime-rich soil.

A mire bouquet: *Selaginella selaginelloides*, the Spatulate Sundew, *Drocera linearis*, and dwarfed Pitcher Plant, *Sarracenia purpurea*. Dorcas Bay, Bruce Peninsula, Ont. 17 July 1977

Cedar Lowland and Stream

In the region of sedimentary bedrock that makes up much of the Great Lakes Basin, swamps and low streamsides often grow pure stands of the White Cedar, Thuja occidentalis. This chapter is based on the woods along the Speed River, northwest of Oustic, Eramosa Township, Ontario.

Within the cedar forest's heavy shade, tall trunks clothed softly in stringy pale-gray bark stand in cloisters. Their naked lower branches, sweeping across the spaces between, lace the gloom as if with giant, gray spider webs. Here and there sunlight pierces evergreen boughs and latticed branches above you, barring the shade with hazy golden light, accenting the crisscrossing of fallen branches on the rusty brown carpet of cedar litter. Like all evergreens in cool climates, the White Cedar drops its older leaves and twigs in the autumn. Last fall, flat tough leaves of interlocking scales that had lived from two to five years lightened to orange, became dry and brittle, and fell. New growth came in the spring at the ends of the leafy branches, glossy and bright golden-green.

       Chattering a call like castinets, a Kingfisher glides on smoke-blue wings from the tip of a cedar to perch on the bare branch of a dead elm, and then swoops off again, over the stream, watching for a chance to dive for a fish, frog or crayfish. Other birds call — Crows cawing in the distance, a nuthatch's nasal call, and the warbling music of Purple Finches — but through all the sounds of the forest runs the stream, speaking with many voices according to its riffles and eddies.

opening
spring buds
ooze
sticky,
spicy-
smelling
sap.

Balsam Poplar.
Populus balsamifera

female flower, "catkin"

At the edge of a sandbar, a Robin flutters and splashes and dips, its bath like a shower. In the lee of driftwood held by the water-washed roots of a curved old cedar, the sunlit, golden-stoned stream bed is alive with wavering networks of ripple-shadows and ripple-light. Over the bottom, close to the bank, scoot torpedo-shaped shadows surrounded by round dark spots, made by iridescent-sided water striders. These are long-legged bugs that skate on the dimples their feet make in the surface tension. They chase after small flying insects that hover to lay their eggs in the water, and will grab anything that blows onto the surface or falls from the bank: ants, gnats, aphids, or leafhoppers. Minnows keep an eye on the water striders, and are just as ready to snatch a tidbit from the grasp of the striders as from the surface itself. If you wade slowly, barelegged in the stream, feet stirring up the bottom, and then stand still, you will be tickled by the quick nips of small fish, striking at bits of sediment which settle on your skin.

When turning rocks in search of crayfish, and sculpins, the beautiful, large-finned, bottom-feeding fish, you should also carry a clear glass jar in which to examine smaller stream dwellers. See how caddisfly larvae have built tubes of wood or sand, which they carry about with them for shelter; how dragonfly nymphs fold their large jaws beneath their chests; and how aquatic snails have their eyes at the base of their tentacles. Find small cone-shelled limpets; the flat beetle larvae called

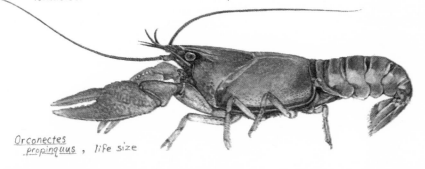

Orconectes propinquus, life size

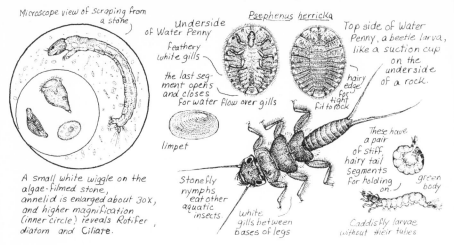

Microscope view of scraping from a stone

Underside of Water Penny
feathery white gills
the last segment opens and closes for water flow over gills

limpet

Psephenus herricka

Top side of Water Penny, a beetle larva, like a suction cup on the underside of a rock.
hairy edge for tight fit to rock

These have a pair of stiff hairy tail segments for holding on.
green body

A small white wiggle on the algae-filmed stone, annelid is enlarged about 30×, and higher magnification (inner circle) reveals Rotifer, diatom and Ciliate.

Stonefly nymphs eat other aquatic insects
white gills between bases of legs

Caddisfly larvae without their tubes

water pennies; leeches that whip about, and fasten with tail sucker to the glass; and tiny, gray, paper-thin flatworms that glide up the side, so that you can see their feeding parts in mid-body, and the eyespots in their heads.

Where the stream banks are vertical, and the soil is held from crumbling into the stream by a network of tough cedar roots, Muskrats make their burrows, and you may glimpse, nearby, the movement of a sleek brown shape, propelled by a strong, gray tail, the force of the water pushing bubbles of air from its waterproof fur as it swims against the current. Mammals of the forest are also seen at the stream, especially in early morning and evening, when deer drink, foxes and weasels hunt, and Raccoons forage.

Deep in the darkest, wettest part of the cedar forest, Hemlock trees spread their feathery boughs, and woodfern graces the shadows. The small, lobed leaves of Herb Robert and Wild Geranium twinkle against damp black earth. Crystal clear water wells out of holes in the bottoms of little pools where tiny free-living nematode worms writhe in a perpetual dance of life. Here, White-tailed Deer take refuge from hunters in the fall. You will find the forest path chopped up by the sharp hooves of White-tailed Deer, and perhaps notice a willow by the stream with its trunk scraped bare of bark by the antlered assault of a buck in rutting fever. The bucks are itching to fight in the fall, for this is mating time, and timid bucks are chased away from the does. Another mammal sign that you may find, always near the stream, is grass flattened in one direction, a sort of drag path winding about among the aspens. Look for the pointed stumps of felled trees, bearing broad, clean beaver-tooth cuts. The paths are made by the Beavers as they drag branches and sticks to the stream. The lodge, a dome of sticks and mud, is separate from the dam. Its doorway is underwater, below winter ice level in this pond that the Beavers have made in the stream.

As the water cools, cold-blooded animals become more sluggish, and move into deeper water where they will be less likely to be locked into winter ice. The chemistry of their body fluids changes to prevent the cell-shattering effects of water freezing within themselves, since the fast-flowing water beneath the ice will drop to temperatures below freezing.

Through the winter, the stream forms many layers of ice as its level fluctuates in response to thaws and cold snaps. Looking between the layers where ice has broken, you can see splendid crystal caverns hung with icicles and shelved with thin glassy lace. While snowshoeing or skiing on the winding, snow-blanketed winter stream, you meet patterns that show where weasel, Mink, Cottontail Rabbits, and Snowshoe Hares crossed the stream, or where a fox trotted along it. Tracks made by webbed feet and dragging tails in the soft snow over the beaver dam show that the Beavers are up and about to supplement their winter food stores from trees felled in the autumn.

When winter's grip is loosed and the final thaw turns ice and snow to water, the stream swells to a torrent. It shifts fallen trees; undercuts banks; and piles gravel and driftwood on sandbars and against resisting roots and jammed logs. Brown and turbid, it flattens the grass on the banks and spreads among the trees, drifting leaf litter and land snail shells.

After the flood subsides, Marsh Marigold blooms first, on fresh black river-borne silt, in bouquet-like bunches of bright yellow flowers surrounded in startling green by large round leaves. Violets grow close beneath the cedars and on the path, gleaming purple from the short-bladed grass. Fiddleheads unroll their light green nobs of embryonic fern frond, and in patches of sunlight, orange-flowered jewelweed appears, with delicate jumbles of soft oval leaves, soothing when crushed and rubbed on nettle stings and insect bites. In open spaces between cedar trees, thorny red raspberry bushes, trimmed to snow level by rabbits during the winter, sprout many new shoots. While Pussy Willows swell velvety silver catkins and the poplars scent the spring breeze with their sticky fragrant buds, the Ruffed Grouse, crop stuffed with catkins, drums on a log. He sounds like a tractor motor that starts sluggishly, picks up speed, thrums up to a dead stop, and begins again. The female grouse, picking at this and that on the ground, may be quietly impressed but, if she is, she shows no sign of it.

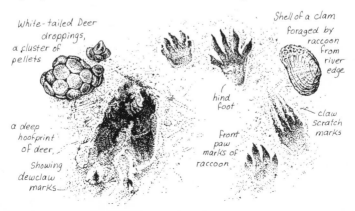

White-tailed Deer droppings, a cluster of pellets

a deep hoofprint of deer, showing dewclaw marks

hind foot

Front paw marks of raccoon

Shell of a clam foraged by raccoon from river edge

claw scratch marks

Eastern Cattail Marsh

This chapter is based on marshes in southern and eastern Ontario; similar marshes occur west to the prairies and well north into the boreal forest in Canada and the northeastern United States.

In the springtime, the marsh retains the tan color of last year's cattails. This year's stand is only showing its tips; tender green spears rising clean from their mucky winter bed of cattail roots and rhizomes. Pull up a bright baby shoot. Bite it, and you'll share with the Muskrat smoothness and crispness together, the very freshness of spring. But the Muskrat doesn't stop at shoots. It eats rhizomes below the winter ice, feeds on summer stems and leaves, and builds its house out of light, strong stalks in the fall. You may see the Muskrat swimming, with only its blunt head breaking the surface. Look out for another one hunched in the shallows a little way off, munching a clam or crayfish. Even if you don't happen to see this fat, furry mammal, you can be sure he is there, because he is as much a part of this place as the cattails and the Redwing Blackbirds, and his droppings, cattail cuttings, and heaps of opened clams are all about.

The spring and summer blackbird makes quite sure that you know he is there, and that he thinks you shouldn't be. Nothing that moves should be in his territory, and especially near the nests of his wives. When a female isn't on the nest or foraging for insects and snails, she may be just as loud and fierce as her mate, though her brown-streaked plumage is less impressive than the male's glossy black with bright shoulder patches.

The air is filled with strident blackbird voices. Passionate bundles of black and red feathered aggression chase each other on the wing, clash in fights, and shout challenges from every corner of the best and biggest patches of marsh they can keep. Weaklings and latecomers who are driven from the marsh go to defend territories in meadow or brush, where they will breed if females accept their properties. A century ago, Redwings nested only in marshes, but now they often use these other habitats.

"Burgalee!" shouts a Redwing from a cattail stem quite close as you pass. Stop there and he won't fly away. He just shifts his position on the stem to look bigger and blacker, stretches his neck, and shouts again. Cocking his head to see if you have decided to leave yet, he raises his feathers and half spreads his wings to look even larger, and to display the scarlet and yellow wing patch that he keeps mostly covered by his back feathers when he's not feeling saucy.

According to the age and fierceness of males, Redwings can have one to four mates and nests in one territory. In the early spring while there is still snow on the ground and ice on the water, and before any other marsh birds have arrived from the south, the male Redwings arrive in big flocks from the southern and central United States. Many birds, like the Redwing, that are abundant and have different male and female plumages, have separate spring arrival times, so that the males may have an early chance to establish territories — so early that there is very little food to be found; but they manage. Sometimes you see a male Redwing stop his singing for a moment to tear with his bill at the head of the cattail to which he is clinging. He is eating the tiny caterpillars of the Cattail Worm Moth that have been in their silk-lined burrows in the seed heads all winter; there they have cut their way about through the fluff, eating seeds. Female blackbirds arrive later, when the weather is warmer and food is more plentiful, their only consideration being the rearing of young blackbirds.

Grackles come to the marsh shortly after the Redwings. They find places of their own in the trees and bushes. The males are black with a bronzy shine on the back, and with blue iridescence in the glossy head and neck feathers. The charcoal-brown females are dull-feathered and a little smaller. A male Grackle sits with drooped wings in a willow bush. He lifts all his feathers and clucks once to catch anyone's attention. Then he sleeks his plumage, tucks up his wings, and breaks into a phrase of song like a very rusty gate hinge.

Where a road runs through the marsh, the Grackles stay in the

Green Frog

Rana clamitans

sits for his portrait

Muskrat   *Ondatra zibethicus*
swims away
with willow
branch

males
alighting
singing
and
feeding

Redwing
blackbirds
*Agelaius
phoeniceus*

*Bombus
perplexus*

dead
bumblebee

by the
side
of the road

grass by the edge, but the Redwings come right out on the shoulder, searching for the right sizes of grit for their gizzards and for insects that have been hit by cars. I saw a Redwing walking along the roadside on his neat black legs and feet. His black head was down with neck outstretched, searching the sand. He called regularly, a shrill note or two, without even looking up from his inspection of the ground. Two small grasshoppers and a dragonfly were found and eaten, but he walked around the dead bumblebees. I suppose that every young blackbird learns its own lesson about bumblebees; some bees are only stunned, and not as dead as they look.

Now and again a Marsh Wren emits a musically clattering warble. These little brown birds stay deep in the cattails and are rarely seen. The Virginia Rail is also an elusive bird. If you hear a low, short piping call behind a bush or a clump of cattails near the bank, try to locate the sound, and sneak around slowly and quietly in the right direction. Most times you will not see the bird, but only the furtive little movements of something keeping bushes between you and it, still piping away and sounding a bit perturbed, but loth to leave its territory. More patient quiet sneaking may be rewarded by the discovery of an exquisite little rail, all subtly shaded with rich rust, brown, and blue-gray feathers. In early spring its usually chestnut brown bill can be bright scarlet. Rails eat snails and insects that they find in and near the water.

While you are hunting for

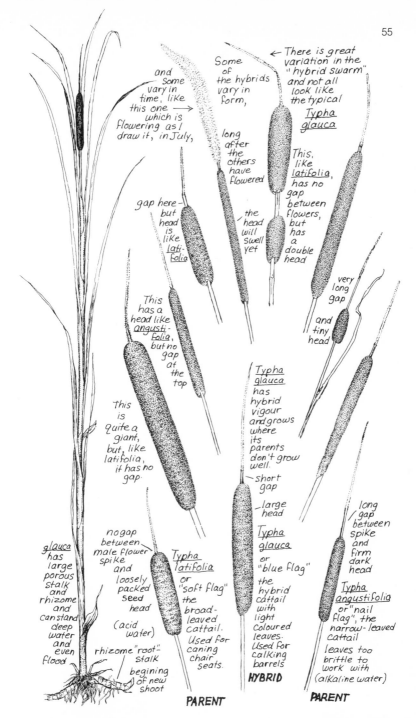

and some vary in time, like this one → which is flowering as I draw it, in July,

Some of the hybrids vary in form,

← There is great variation in the "hybrid swarm" and not all look like the typical *Typha glauca*

long after the others have flowered

This, like *latifolia*, has no gap between flowers, but has a double head

gap here - but head is like *lati-folia*

the head will swell yet

This has a head like *angusti-folia*, but no gap at the top

very long gap

and tiny head

This is quite a giant, but, like *latifolia*, it has no gap.

Typha glauca has hybrid vigour and grows where its parents don't grow well.

short gap

large head

long gap between spike and firm dark head

glauca has large porous stalk and rhizome and can stand deep water and even flood

no gap between male flower spike and loosely packed seed head

(acid water)

rhizome "root"-stalk beginning of new shoot

Typha latifolia or "soft flag" the broad-leaved cattail. Used for caning chair seats.

Typha glauca or "blue flag" the hybrid cattail with light coloured leaves. Used for calking barrels

Typha angustifolia or "nail flag", the narrow-leaved cattail leaves too brittle to work with (alkaline water)

PARENT

HYBRID

PARENT

There are three kinds of cattail in eastern cattail marshes: two parent species and hybrids. After the first generation the hybrids become extremely variable. Lake Scugog, near Port Perry, Ont. July 1975

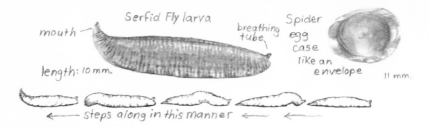

Serfid Fly larva

mouth —

breathing
tube

Spider
egg
case
like an
envelope

length: 10 mm.

11 mm.

←—— steps along in this manner ←—   ←—

sight of a rail, you may startle a green or brown Leopard Frog with light-ringed dark spots. After the splash, watch where it vanishes with two or three strong leg strokes into an underwater maze of brown cattail remains. Or, you may just quietly notice a Green Frog on a lily pad, soaking up as much spring sun as it can through its olive back, which, to absorb more heat from sunlight, gets dark when the frog is cold. A frog's brain is slower then, too, and sometimes you may come near and slowly place your hand right around him before he reacts to your presence. Warm frogs are lighter colored, and since warm muscles and nerves work faster, they are very hard to catch. When the marsh warms under the noon sun, fear of your approach is an excited wave of quick splashes, several meters ahead of you.

Hundreds of tiny tree frogs called Spring Peepers aggregate at the marsh edge before all the snow is gone. They are most active at night, when they advertise their little territories with peeps that are very loud for such a small animal. Males wait for egg-swollen females to come within reach. Then, in the dark, they amplex, the male on the female's back, clasping her tightly behind the arms; when the water is warm enough, the female releases her eggs, and the male his sperm. The eggs are laid singly, and are very hard to find.

Chorus Frogs call day and night, pausing only in the early morning, and for a short while at dusk. "Grrrrrick," like the teeth of a comb, sounds the call of this frog, which is about the same size as the Peeper. Chorus Frogs are dark brown with black spots or stripes. You may find their small masses of jelly-coated eggs stuck to cattail stems underwater.

After the Peepers and Chorus Frogs begin to call, the Leopard Frogs come up from the mud and float silently, waiting. As

Under an old
piece of
bark
from the
ground:

very
visible,
two red
velvet
mites

and nearly invisible,

a carni-
vorous
beetle
larva

the water temperature reaches 12°C, the males call with chugging grunts and snores, "Graow, graow, Kekekekekekekekek." Toads are also early risers. They come from their dry holes in the earth to get cold and wet, and the male shouts his long high trill in the night.

In the late spring the Green Frogs rouse and the male's call is "Gunk," with a falling inflection. He will fight with any yellow-throated frog with a high bearing that comes through the water under his bush. Female Green Frogs have white throats, and stay low in the water. They are tolerated, and eventually amplexed. Latest to breed are the big Bullfrogs, bellowing their well known "Jug-a-rum!" The pitch of the call signals the size of the caller — the lower the pitch the larger the frog. Bullfrogs often come to combat; they wrestle, clasping and straining, and often standing straight up out of the water in their struggle for dominance.

Responding to the changing season, aquatic snails begin to glide gracefully over the mud and vegetation in water that was ice all winter. Succinea snails, lovely jewels of the marsh, climb dry cattail stems, waving tentacled eyes in the sunny spring air. Look closely. Lacy black patterns on the mantle and internal organs show clearly through the amber shell, and a broad, flowing, pale foot carries the body faster than you would expect it to. It loves wet places but, being a land snail, can't hibernate under water; it winters in clumps of grass and mats of dead cattails. A canoe paddled through a marsh in early spring, when the snails are becoming active, may accumulate hundreds of them. From the dry cattails they tumble into the boat like shiny mottled seeds, and crawl about on the outside, above the waterline.

Arachnid life makes its springtime emergence from old logs and bark and from under dead grass. A little red velvet mite is marching through a jungle of long yellow grass and across a bare sunny spot on the high ground. Its path crosses that of a wandering spider, out for a bit of sun and prospecting for a suitable spot in which to spin an insect trap. The landscape has been changed by the winter snow and ice, and the world must now be rediscovered.

By looking closely at a small patch of marsh ground, much can be seen. Springtails will be there. Rabbit-faced, insect-like animals, they have an abdominal segment modified especially for jumping more than a hundred times their own length. Some kinds of springtail are charcoal black, some brown, some yellow, and some are bright metallic violet. All

The leech *Placobdella parasitica* feeds on Snapping Turtles. It can be orange-brown or tawny in color. Pond N of Paudash Lake, Hastings Co., Ont. 4 October 1973

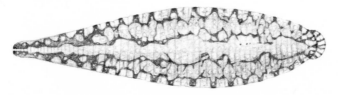

are very small, ranging from a half millimeter to four millimeters in length. The only way to catch them for a closer look is to chase them into a bottle or vial, as fingers are no match for their speed. If you are lucky, one may sit still for a moment beneath your magnifying glass. If you find some tiny pupillid land snails under a log, a magnifying glass will reveal all the smooth perfection of their shells and their delicate dark gray bodies with eye tentacles that pull inside like the finger of a glove.

a *Succineid*
Oxyloma retusa

ram's horn snail

Helisoma trivolvis

this is a land snail

a fingernail clam

lives in mud

Sphaerium

a small *Lymnaea* species

All are water snails except *Oxyloma*

Lymnaea stagnalis

Physa gyrina

Investigation of the smaller marsh life may be interrupted by the sudden clamor of many Redwing voices, and a great rush and clatter, as they all rise in a flock. A Harrier, the source of the shadow which has just passed over, is forced to swerve in the course of its low gliding flight. The mob closes in on him. Rising, he quickens his wingbeat to go away from here and hunt over the fields for mice, in peace. This mob action is useful to Redwings. A hawk that is being driven away can't find nests and eat nestlings, and neither can it hurt the chasers, who are small and quick. The hawk must be dissuaded from doing any successful hunting in this area, or it may come back to hunt fledgeling blackbirds later in the season.

It is good to stand and gaze out over a spring cattail marsh for a long while, soaking in the peace and order, and sensing the life all around: the quickening of the sedge grass sprouting anew at your feet, the sunshine-colored glowing and swelling of the willow buds, and the flit

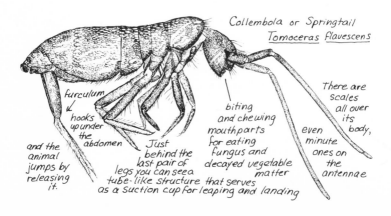

Collembola or *Springtail*
Tomoceras flavescens

furculum

hooks up under the abdomen

and the animal jumps by releasing it.

Just behind the last pair of legs you can see a tube-like structure that serves as a suction cup for leaping and landing

biting and chewing mouthparts for eating fungus and decayed vegetable matter

There are scales all over its body, even minute ones on the antennae

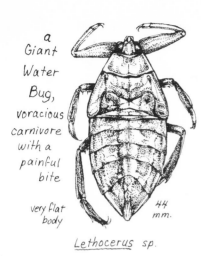

a
Giant
Water
Bug,
voracious
carnivore
with a
painful
bite

very flat
body

44
mm.

Lethocerus sp.

and chip of a Swamp Sparrow near at hand. A distant ripple-wake of a Muskrat moves across a patch of open water. Three or four ducks are out there. One up-ends to dabble in the bottom muck for snails and dragonfly larvae. Another does the same. They pop up, preen, and dabble again. One flaps up from a smooth reflection of the sky, and the others leave in a commotion behind her. Not all the teal have paired off yet, and each single female is followed closely by several males. After chasing back and forth for a while, whistling, squeaking, and quacking, the female in front, they splash down and continue to feed as before. A dark blue patch of ruffled water follows a little wind into the cattails. Water striders scoot between the stems, skating on surface dimples.

Before you turn and go, look again and there may be a Great Blue Heron, coursing with great slow wingbeats across the marsh to a gravelly place where sticklebacks and darters are gathering to spawn.

Great Blue Heron, *Ardea herodias*

Northern Lake

Many lakes were left by the Ice Age glaciers, both where they piled up dams of till, and where they gouged out weak places in the shield, creating lakes with shores of solid rock. The lakes are gradually filling in with bog mat and sediments, forming peaty thickets, marshes, and beaches around their edges. This chapter is based mainly on lakes northeast of Gravenhurst, Muskoka District, and Naiscoot and Harris Lakes, Parry Sound District, Ontario.

In early evening of a damp gray day, a loon call echoes wildly from across the water. Vapors rise into the still, cooling air. As mosquitoes rise also from their secret rain havens, a large dark form moves majestically across the middle of the lake. A young bull Moose, short, blunt antlers still in velvet, stretches head and neck high above the glassy surface. The toes of his large hooves spread as he thrusts his legs through the deep water. Soon he has passed from view into an arm of the lake, and his tracks may be seen, later, showing where he had climbed the bank from the shallow reed-filled bay, and crossed the road. Perhaps he was moving to a sheltered spot to bed down for the night, and along the way, topping off his meal of water lilies with twigs of birch and Balsam Fir. If he had passed near you, it is likely that you wouldn't have noticed, for he places his feet carefully and moves like a whisper. Many times I have risen in the morning to find the tracks of a Moose that had walked through camp only a few meters from me as I slept.

The antlers of Moose are small in comparison to their body size because they spend much of their time in dense forest. Moose antlers are thick and strong for fighting, and broad, like hands, to be visible in threat displays to other males. Both sexes have a pendulous flap of skin under the jaw called the bell, but the male's is larger than that of the antlerless female. She does not need special apparatus for impressing other moose, but only long sharp hooves and powerful forelegs for defence against Wolves. Like all deer, the bulls lose their antlers in late fall. In deep winter, when danger from the cunning of the hungry Wolf pack is greatest, they fight with their hooves.

As you stand over a Wolf track, or even just pause to think about Wolves, you may hear a rustle, or see a movement in the grass at your feet. If you then get a glimpse of a sandy-colored coat and a very long tail, you will know it was a glimpse of a Meadow Jumping Mouse. You may follow it quietly at a discreet distance as it runs in little spurts to the water's edge and without a pause at the brink, swims out quickly to some sedge stems floating on the surface. Watch it cut a seed head and emerge in an instant to perch atop a rock at the water's edge where it

The unionid clam *Elliptio complanata*. Naiscoot Lake, Point au Baril, Parry Sound Dist., Ont. 24 August 1977

turns its complex package over and over, eating the seeds. This mouse is the cause of the grasslike sedge strewn about on the water by the rocks as if someone had been working with a scythe. Perhaps the seeds were not eaten, but packed in its cheek pouches to store safe and dry in its nest. But now the tiny creature with the shiny black hatpin eyes is gone, leaving only some scraps of seed husks.

It sounds as if someone were chopping firewood along the shore, or banging sticks together but, as you listen, the noise seems to come now from this side of the water lilies, and now from the other, over by a big rock. These are the Mink Frogs. They are like Green Frogs, but with flatter heads, more darkly patterned skin, and a musky smell like a mink. The females have creamy bellies, with a little yellow on the chin, while the males' bright buttercup yellow chins and bellies are displayed when they call. Their tadpoles, with large transparent finned tails, are colored much like the adults. They wriggle — round, soft, and slippery like skinned grapes — between the sedge stems as you walk toward them; adults dive with a splash, and kick down into the mud. Raccoons, Mink, Kingfishers, and Great Blue Herons prey on frogs and tadpoles at the lake edge as do the big fish which often come into the shallows from deeper water.

The silent approach and lightning-fast lunge of the long-jawed, speckle-skinned Pike is a selective force which perfects the quick silver dart of minnows, and the elusiveness of Mudminnows, and tadpoles. The smallest fish, sticklebacks, and the several different kinds of minnows, or cyprinids, school in large numbers, warning each other by body movements of the approach of danger. This is so effective as to be instantaneous, and you may see a school of hundreds of slim gray bodies flash silver sides in synchrony and dart in a new direction as if by remote control. When the individuals at the outer edges of the school move in quick alarm, the others see the movement and feel the pressure of the water change along their sensitive lateral lines, and all react in an instant.

In late summer on the lake, mergansers, three-quarters grown, dip and dive after small fish. Sometimes your eye catches the silver glint of a fish lifted for swallowing. The bills of the young are not yet red like that of the accompanying adult. With gray backs and rusty feathered heads and necks, the family of mergansers churns away in a close group, not quite frightened enough to submerge as you approach quietly by canoe.

A stately Blue Heron utters a harsh croak and flaps with slow

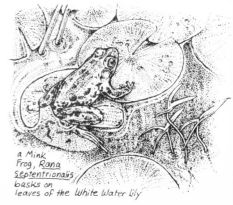

a Mink
Frog, _Rana_
septentrionalis
basks on
leaves of the White Water Lily

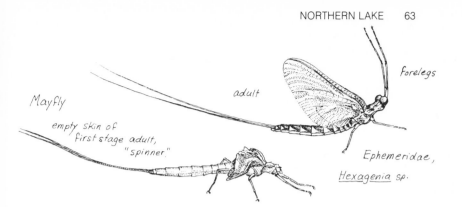

Mayfly

adult

Forelegs

empty skin of
first stage adult,
"spinner"

Ephemeridae,

Hexagenia sp.

grace to a twisted stump where he stands, matching its color as you slip past. His mate, who was crouching on a floating log by the shore, lifts herself and goes on large rhythmic wings to the end of a marshy bay. A loon is confident and curious, but appreciate its elegant black neck and black back patterned with crisp white rectangles while you can, for in a moment it is under, leaving hardly a ripple. Long minutes later, it coyly surfaces somewhere beside or behind you. The loon knows where the rock-dwelling crayfish, blue-clawed *Orconectes virilis* lurks. It knows where long heavy water lily roots lie, like alligators in the mud, and especially where young bass and sunfish hide among the stems of the arrow-leaved *Sagittaria* and in the shadow of floating lily pads, feeding on invertebrates which shelter on the undersides of leaves. Turn back the leaves yourself, and see the diversity of life, from algae to insect larvae, clinging or feeding on the quiet, sun-warmed leaf bottom. You may find clear clusters and strands of snail eggs, and perhaps a jellylike colony of bryozoans, tiny animals with tentacles. The colony grows new members at each end, and slides very slowly along the surface of the leaf.

Your paddle brushes "water clouds," colonial green algae called *Cosmocladium*, some measuring more than a half meter across, hanging

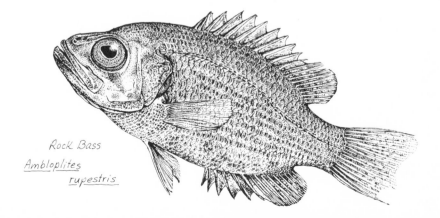

Rock Bass
*Ambloplites
rupestris*

fluffy and translucent in mid-water near the shore. Surrounded by clear, soft jelly, the chlorophyll-bearing algae cells are connected to each other by long thin filaments, increasing the firmness of their large globular colony.

Water grasses lie languidly along the surface, where fierce carnivorous whirligig beetles, like shiny black bubbles, row crazy zigzags here and there, followed by shiny wakes, so that the whole scene resembles an aerial view of berserk speedboats.

Sometimes the sky darkens with cloud, shadowing the water, and a wind rises, chopping the gentle surface into restless motion, and you must leave the lake. If you pull up on a narrow sandy beach, examine what the waves have brought. Before you go, take a souvenir: a hollow dry crayfish claw, perhaps torn off in a fierce fight, now faded to pale pink; clam shells, some dulled by sand and water, others fresh with pearly inner nacre, while the battered outside shows how the shell was eroded during the life of the clam; or strange smooth shapes of drifted wood, subtly carved by sand and water. Oval *Physa*, tall-spired *Lymnaea*, and round "rams-horn" *Helisoma* make up the larger kinds in drifts of empty snail shells lodged among scraps of *Scirpus* and cattail stems.

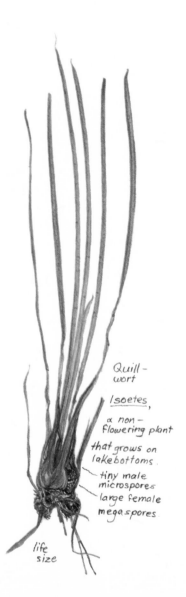

Quill-wort

Isoetes, a non-flowering plant that grows on lakebottoms.

tiny male microspores

large female megaspores

life size

Bare Rock Shield

The Canadian shield is a vast plate of ancient rock extending over most of north central and eastern Canada and the adjacent United States. It has not been disturbed by continental drifting or rifting since the Precambrian. Through the ages, erosion has stripped it down to crystalline igneous and metamorphic rocks which formed in intense heat far below the surface: granite, gneiss, and schist. Most recently it was scraped clear of overlying soil and sedimentary rock by glaciers so that over large areas bare rock is exposed. This chapter is based mainly on the region between Parry Sound and Sudbury, Ontario.

Striding over bare rock that is thinly splotched with lichens in some places, you can see the way in which the hot rock flowed long ago and cooled in curves and ridges, leaving hard bands of granite and pink and white quartz or you may walk over rocks that contain microscopic fossils of some of the oldest forms of life known. The rock may be scored by glacier tracks, long, straight grooves and scratches made by stones carried on the bottom of the steadily moving ice. The solid rock of the shield continues to weather as water gradually penetrates the surface layers, changing the chemical nature of the rock and swelling it until it separates from harder layers underneath. You may hear hollowness under your steps in some places, and see scattered slabs and thin sheets of granite that have been pried off by the pressure of water freezing in the spaces. This process is hastened by lichens, spongelike in their absorbency, which are present on all but freshly exposed rock. In reality, there is little bare rock on the shield. The only rock surfaces free

Showy spore capsules of the moss *Splacknum rubrum*, which grows only on Moose dung. Pukaskwa National Park, Algoma Dist., Ont. July 1977

of this living skin are those which are not exposed to light and air, and those in regions with chemically polluted atmosphere.

The aspect of bare rock shield country is that of a giant park or garden, with trees, shrubs, patches of moss, isolated areas of grass and flowers, small shallow ponds, flat walkways, and great carved stones. But the terrain was carved by glaciers, not arranged by man; and the vegetation grows, each kind where it can, not where a gardener thought it would look best.

Jack Pines, with their rough, contorted branches bristling with short, stiff needles, are intolerant of shade and take advantage of areas with meagre soil, uncrowded by other trees. They bear small, solid cones that open in extreme heat to release light, broad-winged seeds. For many years after a burn, great tracts of the shield are treed exclusively by stunted Jack Pine and sprawling prickly juniper bushes, clouded with pale blue berries. The juniper and the tangle-twigged, small-leaved blueberry often spread in extensive mats, helping to hold a layer of soil over bedrock.

Between the boreal and deciduous forests, the shield bears Red Pines, tall straight trees with thin, flaky, pinkish-brown bark. Their full tufts of long needles are yellower and their limbs shorter than those of the White Pines that grow with them. Red Pines are especially good at wedging their long tough roots deep into cracks in the bedrock, and flourish, growing especially tall around lakes.

Two dominant kinds of reindeer moss grow here in loose, spongy rounded patches, one pale sulphur yellow, and the other grayish, greenish white. Drifted pine needles line the cracks of exposed rock, and border patches of vegetation. The bright green growing tips of Hair Cap Moss star the brown background of its other years' growth, surprisingly thick and cushiony against hard rock. Many fungi can be found nestled in mats of moss and lichen, feeding on buried needles and fallen twigs. A long mound of deep moss, full frothy lichens, and clumps of tall grasses was perhaps begun long ago by the rotting of a fallen tree. A young Pin Cherry tree with smooth, long, flexible leaves and lenticel-marked satiny red bark has made a good start there.

In a thickly moss-floored hollow, shaded by a tall White Pine, the Bracken seems to stand aside for a large congregation of *Maianthemum* leaves, glowing in the sunshine like little green lanterns. Round firm white berries with wine red speckles are clustered at the top of each solitary flower stalk. The leaves are narrower and more upright than those of the *Maianthemum* of western forests. Rock Tripe lichen plasters a shaded rock wall with large, smooth, grayish-olive flakes like old leaves, each fastened tightly to the granite with a short, strong central stipe. A cluster of leathery-leaved *Polypodium* ferns writhe, fresh and green from a clutter of dry fronds. The felt cocoons of caterpillar pupae are fastened to the sides of dark spider-silk-laced cracks.

Like its horizontal limbs, the root system of White Pine is broad and spreading, enabling survival where the soil above bedrock is shallow or poorly drained. Red Squirrels cut long green cones from the windy tops of White Pines. They drop with heavy thumps on the needle-sprinkled moss. Closed tightly, unripe, and scattering no seeds, the cones will be buried in caches for winter use. Hummingbirds swoop and buzz, iridescent feathers glinting in the sun. They are insect-catching for their young, and only occasionally hover to sip nectar from purple asters, Pale Corydalis, and pink Wintergreen flowers. A gray-breasted, brown-backed Song Sparrow cocks a pert striped head and pecks at something in the grass — perhaps the little black crickets that sprang and scurried into the curly-leaved grass bases as you walked there. Busy dark brown ants are everywhere, continually investigating their small familiar territories for food.

Where rainwater collects on the hard rock of the shield, bladderwort fills the water with green bottlebrush branches, and black dytiscid beetles dive, the predators of mosquito larvae. Sedges spike the pale clay of the gradual margin, and fragrant bushy Sweetfern thrives on the surrounding thin moist soil.

Lichens: Powdery white *Crocynia membranacea,* ripply *Parmelia cumberlandiana*, green mosaic Map Lichen, *Rhizocarpon geographicum,* spongy *Cladonia mitis*, Pixie Trumpet and *Cladonia chlorophaea,* and a newly transformed toad, *Bufo americanus*. Harris Lake, 65 km N of Parry Sound, Ont. 26 August 1977

Lesser Yellowlegs, *Tringa flavipes*.
Near Vee Lake, Yellowknife, N.W.T. 18
June 1975

A slim young garter snake silently slips over the rock from the dark base of a Juniper into the sunshine, and stops, head alertly poised, and soft red and black tongue flicking. It hunts for grasshoppers and crickets in the grass and catches small frogs at the edges of rainwater pools.

After a rain, the long, twisting, branching tangles of *Cladonia*, once crunchy and breakable, spring back softly from your steps, and the colors of encrusting lichens glow, fresh and bright, against the dark wet rock. Now you notice the multitude of lichen forms. Sea green Pixie Trumpets, tubes with cupped tops, poke from their coral-like, crinkly green clutter which covers old White Pine needles and dusts more recent needles with pale green velvet. Frothy piles of powdery asbestos gray lichen perch here and there, delicately and evenly supported by smooth creamy veins underneath. Another lichen encrusts the rock like splashes of dull green or gray paint with dark circles within, as if it had fallen on a wet surface. Shapeless, floppy, army-green flakes like torn bits of weather-curled rubber attach imperceptibly as if lying loose on the already untidy rock surface. Velvety mounds and lumps of gray-green spread like bread mold on their rock, bubbling up and trapping any soil that might wash beneath them. Cracked brown patches like old, dried pea soup form a thin, crusty, inconspicuous layer of living cells over the hard mineral surface. Others grow in that form: a yellow-green lichen, geometrically divided by minute cracks, its largest sections bearing black central pits for spore production, and a dull reddish-brown lichen in a miniature tile-work of tightly clustered, minutely black-speckled lumps. A distinct part of the overall landscape, frilly greenish-white encrusting lichens splay in bold rings and round patches on the smooth massive forms of rocks. Their perimeters are fresh and bright as the chalky ripply ribbons of lichen body lengthen and branch slowly outward. In the cold northern parts of the shield, bluffs and boulders are painted brilliantly by hardy orange, black, and yellow lichens, so that long-exposed rock, although often bare of soil and vascular plants, is never quite naked.

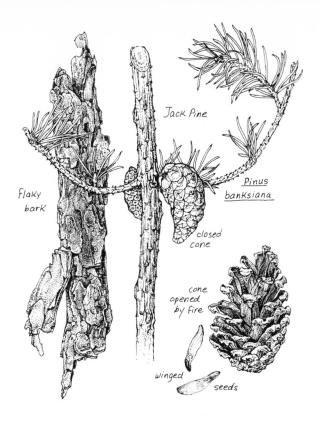

Jack Pine

Pinus banksiana

flaky bark

closed cone

cone opened by fire

winged seeds

Burn

Large parts of the boreal forest have long dry seasons, and burn often in fires started either by lightning or people. This chapter is based on a number of burns north of Opasatika, Cochrane District, and near Gogama, Sudbury District, Ontario.

Where the fire began it bared the soil of both growing and dead ground cover, and littered it instead with ash and broken, partly burned branches. The tree trunks are completely blackened only at the bottom, burned thoroughly as the fire consumed the forest floor. Higher, among dead branches, the flames climbed more rapidly. There it turned patches of bark into brittle flakes of charcoal, and left much untouched in its haste to snatch crackling, snapping, resiny needles. Often a strong wind is generated by a big fire, whether on a windy day or not, and burning branches are tossed up with the smoke and hot air across the tops of trees, so the fire rushes ahead of itself, a crown fire, spreading quickly for great distances in the top of the forest.

Have you ever considered whether perhaps those vast tracts of highly flammable trees were that way on purpose? Shade-intolerant Black Spruce and Jack Pine cannot outshade other trees, and their seedlings must have full sun to grow. By being full of resin, clothed in flaky, tinder-dry bark, and littered all about with light, dry twigs and needles, these trees are well equipped to burn everything down. Their cones stretch wide in the searing dragon-breath of the fire, and their light, broad-winged seeds escape, borne far and high in the hot smoky wind, to land eventually on cooling ashes, and germinate after the next drenching rain.

After the fire, what's left is a burn. Little puffs of ash fly up around your feet at every step, reminiscent of the smoke which only days ago ceased to seep from the charred earth. Smoke is no longer in the air, but the smell of ash lingers. Like great sticks of burned firewood, spruce trunks lie across one another, burned into half circles where they touched, some notched as if beaver-chewed. Their surfaces are cracked and puffed into a crocodile skin pattern, reflecting the sky like quilted black satin. Where their tips burned away, lie telltale piles of brittle Black Spruce cones. The soil surface is now so black and open to the sun that it is a perfect incubator for growing things, which will thrive on the minerals released by the burning of peat and litter. Herbs and grasses break the blackness with fresh bright tips and tender leaves, some from unburned roots and rhizomes, and some from seeds brought by the wind. Tall spikes of pink flowered Fireweed are named for their habit of moving in after fires, their small light seeds borne from miles away on silky parachutes of fluff. Disturbed from basking, little white moths fly up with the black dust of your footsteps, and dark spiders scurry, white egg capsules glimmering from beneath their lifted abdomens. Dark toads hop under charred branches, but turn pale and lichen-patterned when they shelter under the lacy unburned tangle of fallen spruce tops. The top of a spruce is bushy with small twigs and clotted with little gray cones. Notice how widely the cones are opened, and how seeds flutter from them at the slightest tap.

Spring Peepers sing from isolated bog pools where they took refuge while the fire raged fiercely around them. Here, leaves of Labrador Tea and willow are curled and brittle, breaking and falling at a touch. Along the stream, tussocks of grass which were close to the burning forest stand up from the ash like blackened brooms. Often when a fire comes to a stream it will stay along one bank for miles until wind that it creates blows it across to the trees on the opposite side. Even

New growth, a few days after fire.
14 km N 7 km W of Opasatika,
Cochrane Dist., Ont. 24 June 1977

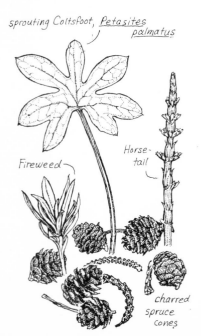

sprouting Coltsfoot, *Petasites palmatus*

Fireweed

Horse-tail

charred spruce cones

where the fire crossed, the banks of the stream may remain unburned, a ribbon of green through the charred wilderness.

Your path among the vanquished trees is well below the original forest floor, perhaps half a meter lower than you would have walked, had you been there before the fire. Beneath some trees you can peer through tangles of exposed roots into caves carved by the smouldering fire. In a boggy forest, *Sphagnum* stands high about the black trunks of spruces in grotesque yellow mounds, like giant ocean sponges, pitted with holes gouged by the burning of fallen twigs. Sculpted like snow when it melts around sun-warmed bark, the moss is scorched away in ringlike depressions about the trunks. The outer *Sphagnum* leaves are evenly singed off, crisp and dry to the touch, but only a millimeter or two inside, it is damp with gallons of water, more water than the fire had fuel to evaporate. Here, toads, spiders, and beetles went to hide. Part the moss, and inside you will find it cool and wet, its slightly greenish color unchanged.

At the grassy forest edge, earth that was deep, damp, and rich with tiny living things is now crumbly, cracked, and dry. In a handful of burned soil you may find several fragile white shells of small land snails. For years the empty shells of snails that lived and died in grass, leaf litter, and rotting wood, remained intact in the soil. Now after the fire, they are delicate coiled forms of white ash, reduced to powder at a touch. Find also, near the surface, brittle, glossy black shells which had been clear and strong, with living animals inside, before they and their habitat were consumed by the passing fire. As you explore the burn you will find remains of vertebrates, too. Most of these are not the bones of animals killed by fire, but old graves of the forest, their coverings burned away. However, many animals are killed by the fire. A fire ranger told me that he had found burned Moose, deer, foxes, Porcupines, and squirrels.

On an unburned, hoary, cone-clotted spruce top, burned away from its fallen trunk, poises the startling form of a long-bodied beetle, funeral black, with one white dot at the base of each hard, finely crinkled wing cover. It slowly sweeps about with extremely long, many-jointed antennae, the bases of which are glowing-ember red in color. This longicorn beetle and its kind have newly emerged from the trees. Roused by the fire's heat, waiting pupae have transformed within dead wood and bored their way with pincer jaws to light, air, and a burned forest. Here you will find them walking slowly about, searching out one another by scent, their business to produce another generation of wood-boring beetles.

A Nighthawk egg, lightly tan-speckled and glossy like polished granite, lies alone on the sooty ground, the ash only slightly disturbed around it. The commotion of a few moments earlier was the mother leaving. Only a few days after the fire, this site was found and nesting begun. You can glimpse an occasional flash of white wing pattern in the evening, as the Nighthawks fly high, scooping insects into their gaping mouths. Their "Peep" call, and the deep buzzing boom of the male, swooping up from his display dive, sound in the darkening light over this blackened land.

Two or three years after the burn, the charcoal is weathering from the dead trees. Now they appear more silver than gray, and the forest

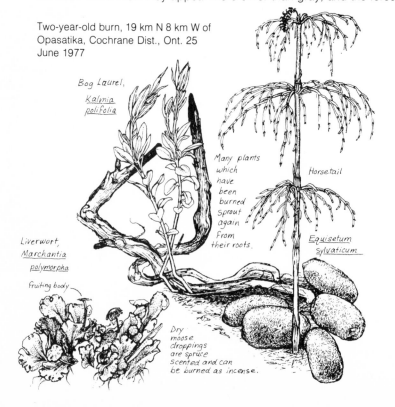

Two-year-old burn, 19 km N 8 km W of Opasatika, Cochrane Dist., Ont. 25 June 1977

Bog Laurel, Kalmia polifolia

Many plants which have been burned sprout again from their roots.

Horsetail

Equisetum sylvaticum

Liverwort, Marchantia polymorpha

fruiting body

Dry moose droppings are spruce scented and can be burned as incense.

regrows at their feet. Fireweed is well established, tall red stems with narrow green leaves. Baby spruces, small enough to step over, grow densely needled and vigorous, with tender tail-like branch tips. The four-leaved Herb Dogwood fills spaces as Lowbush Blueberry, blushing red from lack of shading canopy, spreads with fresh vigor to cover rocky ground. Wintergreen comes too. Its oval leathery leaves, pepsin flavored and almost sweet, are delicious to nibble. Pale Corydalis graces the sunny landscape of new growth with broad delicate blue-green leaves and snapdragonlike flowers of pink and yellow. Drought-tolerant mosses of many kinds begin to cover bare rocky spots, and in the lowland, *Sphagnum* has regrown, soft and pale green. Tiny-leaved cranberry decorates the *Sphagnum*, and Bog Rosemary flourishes in wet places. The lilies, Mayberry and *Clintonia*, grow among shoots of raspberry on higher ground, and small strawberry plants are connected by a network of thin red runners. Birches send forth many little trees about their bases. These trees with their shaggy, highly flammable bark seem to take advantage of fire. After five or six years, Balsam, Poplars, aspen, alders, and willows give the spruces competition, in some places chest-high, and gooseberry, bush dogwood, and ash crowd together, shadowing tall ferns. The new forest grows in a thick tangle, discouraging the traveler on foot. Above, in the tall, thin skeletons of the forest that was before the burn, the wind whistles, haunting and ghostlike.

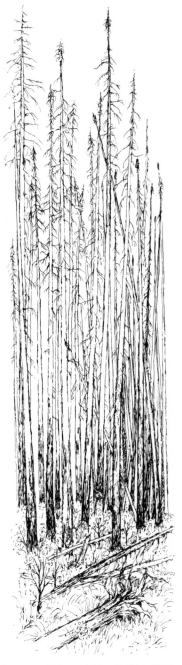

Six-year-old burn. 23 km N 8 km W of Opasatika, Cochrane Dist., Ont. 25 June 1977

Pitcher-
plant

Bog

*Bogs are places where organic matter has accumulated under acid conditions.
Both impeded drainage and low temperature contribute to this accumulation, so
that bog conditions extend through much of the northern boreal forest, but are
increasingly restricted toward the south. Near the southern limits of glaciation bogs
occur only in rare pockets of poor drainage. This chapter is based mainly on bogs
near Cochrane, Ontario; and Cap Lumière, New Brunswick.*

The Black Spruce trees dwindle in size as they close in on the bog. Bog
vegetation glows in rich green and rust through the widening spaces
between them. As you pass the shoulder-high trees, you can hear the
squelch of water somewhere in the peat, at each step. Here the bog mat
is strong and even, sewn together by the tough roots of leathery-leaved
heaths, and compressed by the weight of centuries of water-filled
Sphagnum growth. Softly blended in pink, red, rust, pale green, bright
green, and olive like a deep wool rug of autumn colors, the *Sphagnum*
grows up in pillows around the bases of Bog Rosemary and Labrador
Tea. Moss, sprawling spruce branches, and many-twigged heaths drag
at your feet like deep snow, and your knees must be lifted high for each
step. In places the short spruces grow in dense masses, like snowdrifts,

exhausting to walk through. Eventually all vegetation is no higher than
your knees — even the stunted, sprawling, delicately needled
Tamaracks with gnarled trunks perhaps half a century old. At each step,
water seeps from the moss into a pool around your boot.

Stop then, to rest, for you have probably already walked on many
Pitcher Plants, *Saracenia purpurea*, breaking the stiff red and green
vases that arch up, openmouthed, to trap spiders, ants, and flies. In this
way the Pitcher Plant acquires the nitrogen and phosphorus that it needs
in order to produce its extravagant flower, like a squat, glossy, wax-red
lampshade, turned downward from the top of a tall green stem, as thick
as a pencil.

In bogs isolated from open or running water, there is no teeming
aquatic life — no snails, worms, or crayfish, and no fish — for the acid
water and peat mat lack mineral nutrients necessary to support a
complex food chain. Like many mosses, *Sphagnum* receives all of its
nutrients in rain, which collects small amounts of dust from the
atmosphere. Rain is slightly acid after reacting with carbon dioxide in the
air, but the *Sphagnum* itself produces more acid, to exclude other plants,
making room for more *Sphagnum*. Its cells contain organic acids which
bind minerals, especially calcium and magnesium, and release
hydrogen ions, which make the water so acid that most other organisms
cannot live there. The combination of high acidity and the absence of
oxygen allows only limited decomposition, reducing *Sphagnum* and the
other bog plants to peat. This breakdown produces even more acid, and
the peat itself is preserved. So, through the years, the *Sphagnum*
flourishes and tons of peat are produced, all only partly decomposed,
and then gradually compacted by the weight of the slowly growing bog.
The leaves of *Sphagnum* are only one plant cell in thickness, and are
folded so that they can hold much more water than the weight of each
leaf. So, the deep *Sphagnum* mat, like a giant sponge under a dripping
faucet, stores rainwater well above the surrounding water table. In this
way, bogs sometimes exist on flat rock or even on hillsides. Bog orchids
and heaths have certain fungi that live on or around their roots, helping
them by extracting a little nutrient from the peat.

The bog heaths, Labrador Tea, Leatherleaf, Bog Rosemary, Bog
Laurel, Crowberry, and cranberry all hold their leaves for more than a
year. It would be wasteful to throw away leaves that would only be
preserved by bog water, and not be recycled through decomposition.
Their leathery leaves, like those of some desert plants, allow a minimum
of water loss. The leaves of Bog Rosemary and the pine-and-honey

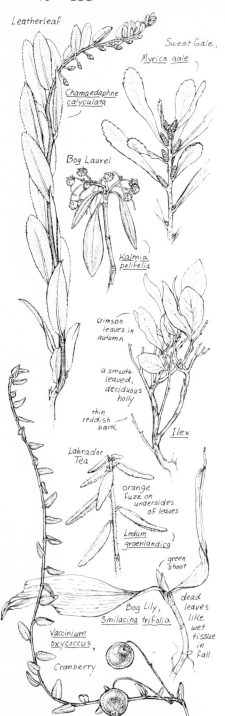

Leatherleaf

Sweet Gale,
Myrica gale

Chamaedaphne calyculata

Bog Laurel

Kalmia polifolia

crimson leaves in autumn

a smooth leaved, deciduous holly

thin reddish bark

Ilex

Labrador Tea

orange fuzz on undersides of leaves

Ledum groenlandica

green shoot

Bog Lily,
Smilacina trifolia

Vaccinium oxycoccus,

Cranberry

dead leaves like wet tissue in fall.

scented Labrador Tea curl under at the edges into almost a cylindrical shape and a dense furriness further protects their respiratory undersides. Cranberry's small, stiff, glossy leaves, spaced alternately on a trailing stem, have rolled edges and a powdery white waxy protection on their undersides. All this is rather surprising in such a wet place, but in winter, while plant roots are frozen fast in ice, water is not available. Should wind rob the heaths of snow cover so that their leaves become active in winter sunshine, photosynthesizing and breathing, they must avoid losing water they cannot replace.

On drier *Sphagnum* mounds, and about the bases of tiny old Black Spruces which dot the bog sparsely like little people's Christmas trees, *Cladonia* lichen grows in hoary clumps. You may find a high brown mound, quite dry and comfortable looking, which ants of the *Formica fusca* complex have built on top of the damp moss using spruce needles and dead Leatherleaf and Bog Rosemary leaves. A few stubby little stems of a Leatherleaf bush stick out from the top. The dead bush helps to support this insect castle in the bog.

As you wander out into the center of the bog, the mat quakes in gentle undulations. There is dark, silent water beneath the peat. In places, the mat sinks under you like an old waterlogged boat. The trampoline action of the bog mat transmits your footsteps to nearby trees, waving them from side to side, and bouncing them up and down. If you see open water, don't venture too near. The mat is likely to be younger and thinner where it slowly grows over the water. This may be a place where the bog mat has sunk, or been torn somehow, or it may even be the last open water of what used to be a lake or a pond.

As bogs grow older they may become so full of peat that in their highest parts, especially around the edges, the mat becomes drier. When air is allowed to get in, peat decomposition begins, and plant roots can penetrate deeper without being drowned. Leatherleaf, Labrador Tea, and spruce grow taller and fuller, starving the *Sphagnum* for light. When the peat breaks down, minerals are released, soil is formed, and a forest grows where there was a bog before.

So bogs disappear, but they also invade, spreading for miles through boreal forest, killing lowland tracts of Black Spruce. At the bog edges, *Sphagnum* makes such an acid environment that the neighboring plants die, and leave room for more *Sphagnum*. Thus conditions are created in which no plants can live except bog plants. Shade-tolerant species of *Sphagnum*, creeping into the forest, collect water and kill the trees by drowning their roots. In muskeg, the expansion of freezing water in winter heaves the bog up in long ridges which eventually support strings of trees, giving the terrain an irregular corduroy appearance, and maintaining an equilibrium between bog and forest.

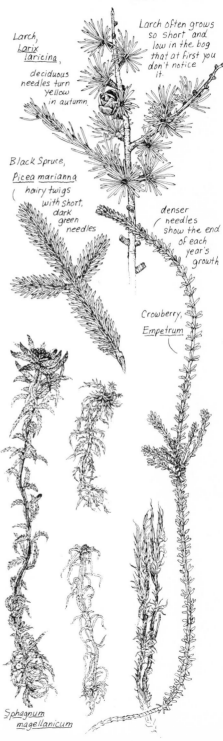

Larch, _Larix laricina_, deciduous needles turn yellow in autumn.

Larch often grows so short and low in the bog that at first you don't notice it.

Black Spruce, _Picea mariana_ (hairy twigs with short, dark green needles

denser needles show the end of each year's growth

Crowberry, _Empetrum_

Sphagnum magellanicum

Tundra

The tundra is a great variety of plant communities that grow on permanently frozen ground between the boreal forest and the limit of plant growth. In North America it covers all of the Arctic Archipelago and vast areas of the mainland in Labrador, northwest of Hudson's Bay, and around Alaska to the Aleutian Islands. This chapter is based on observations made on the Cumberland Peninsula of Baffin Island; and in Churchill, Manitoba.

Lying on a flat place of dry tundra or sitting against a hummock for a near ground level view across the dry tundra, you will find that only rocks rise above the narrow seed heads of hardy summer grasses. The strong, twisted gray trunk by your side does not aspire to height and, if you can forget the scale of the world where trees are tall, you will respect this willow as an old and great tree, telling the tundra story of more than a hundred springs.

You are sitting on trees — willows that are not even the shape of bushes but part of the herb mat itself. With shiny, crinkly, oval leaves and large pink catkins, they push their way through moss and lichens to share the sunlight during long summer days. The willows and heaths here grow slowly, because warmth, water, and nutrients are of limited supply. The low, thickly tangled plant community crowds its branches, twigs, and evergreen leaves into a dense mat, insulating itself from the freezing temperatures which are frequent during the short summer. Here there is little rain. Most of the precipitation falls in winter as snow and, in summer, plants which do not have access to a continuing supply of snow meltwater live in desert conditions.

In moist depressions and in the shelter of cliffs, bluffs, and boulders, shrubby birches and gnarled bushes of willow spread their branches in low domed shapes. Their profiles trace the height and

the
arctic
willow

Salix
arctica

Lupinus arcticus

grows with
grasses

tough
little
leaves
and a
delicate
flower

Dryas integrifolia

Stellaria

an early
spring
flower

Saxifraga oppositifolia

Moss
Campion

Silene
acaulis

placement of the snowdrifts that protected them from extreme winter cold and wind. With them, in this ideal microhabitat, grow Crowberry, the purple-flowered evergreen *Phyllodoce*, labrador tea, low, tangled Cranberry and Bilberry mat, and patches of reindeer moss lichen. All are bedded in a fine tangled layer of roots and stems, dead and alive, and packed all through with mosses.

Where snow is swept from the rocks by wind, or where it melts early on hilltops and high, flat ground, the terrain is barren except for a few lichens, notably the yellow *Cetraria nivalis*. In the shelter of boulders there, the early, pink-flowered *Saxifraga oppositofolia* grows alone in sparse, sprawling mats on sand and gravel. On dry slopes where the snow melts early, the herb mat is very low and thin. Yellow-flowered *Dryas integrifolia* is well adapted for drought with tough, shiny little evergreen leaves, thickly massed together in isolated patches.

As the edges of deep snowdrifts melt in spring and summer, they expose the glossy dark green foliage of *Cassiope tetragona*, a white-flowered bell heather, which needs the moisture of the melting snow. Later melting reveals small, light green pairs of round Herb Willow leaves, with wet-loving saxifrages, fast-growing Dwarf Buttercups, sorrel, dandelions, and a few small grasses. Briefly uncovered by the last of the drifts, and always quite wet, are the dark green spikes of the sedge *Luzula*. Where the snow melts the latest, some very short mosses and a film of algae may cover the otherwise bare wet soil. So, even after the last of the snow has gone in late summer, the patterns of the plants tell where it has been, and for how long.

Above the unyielding frozen ground called permafrost, the soil softens in spring and flows slightly down slopes, settling in a pattern of gentle, regular ribs and grooves. Often the slightly moister grooves can be distinguished from the ridges by a difference in the tone and texture of plant life. *Cassiope* darkens the grooves there, and also in the moist cracks of tundra polygons, which are kept open by water seepage and autumn freezing. In wet meadows, "tussocks" of ground are forced up by the expanding of freezing water in the surface of the meadow. These elevations support mosses, lichens, and many plants of the dry heath. Around and between the tussocks grow the wet-tolerant mosses, the fluffy flowered sedge called cotton grass, and the short sedge *Luzula*.

In spring, the tundra is alive with birds that migrate from the south to breed. Plovers, godwits, phalaropes, jaegers, Horned Larks, Redpolls, Lapland Longspurs, Snow Buntings, and Savannah, Tree, and Harris sparrows are only a few of the many birds which come from the south for the short tundra summers. The birds which live in the tundra year-round are few. These are Rock and Willow ptarmigans, eaters of twigs, buds, and seeds, the scavenging Raven, and two birds of prey, the Snowy Owl and the Gyrfalcon.

In the lee of a large boulder, flatly decorated by gracefully twined willow branches, a ptarmigan has left a handful of light, dry, curved droppings. Near the rock you may also find owl pellets, chunks of silvery gray matted hair, feathers, and small whole lemming bones, regurgitated by Snowy Owls as they sat there watching the tundra. The droppings of Arctic Foxes contain bones as well, but crushed by the foxes' teeth, and not as easy to identify. Caribou bones and antlers, and even the ribs and vertebrae of sea mammals dragged by Wolves or foxes to seaside tundra, are spotted easily as they lie where meals were finished long ago. Animal remains decompose slowly in this cold, dry habitat, and are visible, stark and white, for years while the herb mat slowly closes over them.

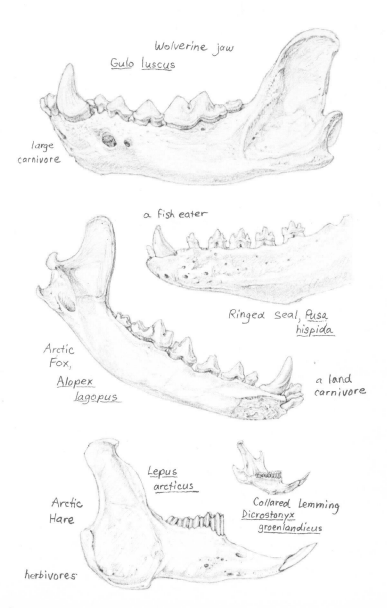

Wolverine jaw
Gulo luscus

large carnivore

a fish eater

Ringed seal, Pusa hispida

Arctic Fox, Alopex lagopus

a land carnivore

Lepus arcticus

Arctic Hare

Collared Lemming
Dicrostonyx groenlandicus

herbivores

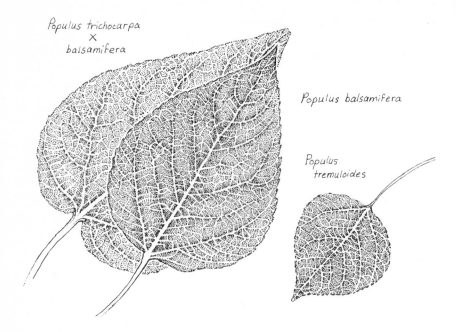

Populus trichocarpa
X
balsamifera

Populus balsamifera

Populus tremuloides

Aspen Parkland

Aspen Parkland is an area of transition between forest and grassland. It lies in a broad band from southern Manitoba through central Saskatchewan and Alberta, north of the great plains and south of the boreal forest. Where this transition occurs in the eastern prairies of the United States, it is dominated by oaks and hickories instead of aspens.

Standing at the edge of an aspen grove, looking out across the sunbathed grasses under the vast, bright blue prairie sky, you see other groves of aspens as shallow domes of dark green, like islands in a broad sea of grass.

While the prairie surrounding the trees looks like a monotonous carpet of paler green or gold, it is really a community of many forms of grass and great diversity of brightly flowered herbs. Grasses are able to bind the soil into a continuous sod which soaks up rain like a sponge. At the edge of the dry prairie, where enough rain falls for trees to grow, they can only survive in close stands, too shady for the grasses. If a grass sod was made beneath the trees, it would rob their soil of water. In the same way that grasses grow together to keep the trees out, the trees grow together to keep the grass out.

Animals that eat plants do well in grassland conditions. Insects and small mammals are sheltered in the close stand of grasses and soft,

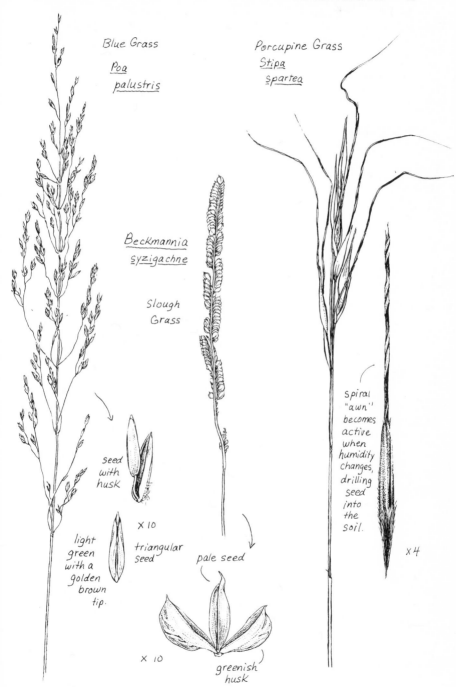

Blue Grass
Poa
palustris

Porcupine Grass
Stipa
spartea

Beckmannia
syzigachne

Slough
Grass

seed
with
husk

X 10

light
green
with a
golden
brown
tip.

triangular
seed

pale seed

X 10

greenish
husk

spiral
"awn"
becomes
active
when
humidity
changes,
drilling
seed
into
the
soil.

X 4

deep soil, and there is an ample food supply for all. Plant diversity is encouraged because there are so many different herbivores. Where a patch of one kind of plant has been eaten, other species may fill its place. Plants which put a lot of their energy into producing poisons or growing spines to avoid being eaten, grow well where they can find gaps among the grasses. Roses, goldenrod, thistles, sage, everlasting, and bergamot are among those that break the fine texture of grass blades and seed heads.

In a series of dry years, aspen groves recede from their edges as the surrounding grassland competes for water. Prairie fires burn through the ground-shading bushes of Snowberry, Saskatoon, and willow at the edges of the aspen groves, clearing the ground there for grasses to grow among the outermost trees and further deprive them of water. In wet years, the forest rebounds. Shrubs advance from its margins, finding plenty of water in spite of the grass, which will eventually die for want of light. As young aspens spring from the tree roots and rapidly outgrow the bushes, the margins of the forest are extended.

Within the edge of the grove rises a rich green undergrowth of Saskatoon bushes, roses, prickly gooseberries, alders, and Fireweed. It may seem rather densely tangled and forbidding to you, but everything around you is at home. A glint of yellow, like sunshine falling on a Saskatoon bush, betrays the presence of a shy Yellow Warbler with buttercup breast and olive yellow back as it gleans insects from the leaves and branches of the undergrowth. Another, invisible in the tangle of Saskatoons, extends a short, warbling, twittering call, and then waits, silent, for an answer.

When you have pressed through the undergrowth into the cool domain of the aspen grove, slim, ghostly tree trunks confront you. All are black-marked with old scars and branch traces, and are startling in their sameness, as if they were all vertical branches of a large prostrate tree. You will find them in groups or clones, the trees of each having similar bark texture, trunk shape, and branching patterns. They even flower, leaf, and drop their leaves in unison as one tree.

X ¾

Bufo boreas, the western toad, has its eastern range limit in Alberta. Unlike the eastern species of Bufo, it prefers walking to hopping.

The Yellow-bellied Sapsuckers regard the aspen trunks as intimately as you would know your own back garden or the cupboards in your kitchen. They punch rows of round holes in the smooth misty gray-green bark. Returning later, they eat insects attracted to the fresh sap, and drink some of the sap themselves. As they move quietly up and around the trunks, the ends of their stiff tail feathers brace against the bark, supporting them. Sometimes you will hear them, briskly hammering new holes, or screaming harsh sapsucker calls as they fly to and fro among the trees.

a Geometrid caterpillar imitating the twig of a saskatoon bush.

× 1¼

To a male kingbird, each tree is either within his territory, on the border, or outside. Not only is the position of each tree in his territory well known, but also the placement of each of its lower branches, whether useful for perching in display, or for perching in wait for large flying insects to capture in flight. Kingbirds are pugnacious, and the very sight of a neighbor is an excuse to chase and chatter and peep, with crest raised, wings flipping, and white feather tips flashing.

Try to check your direction in the forest by carefully noticing the patterns of moss growth on the trees. The sides which are consistently mossier should be facing north. More reliable is the aspen bark itself. The chalky, whitish surface of the smooth, yellow-green bark is thicker

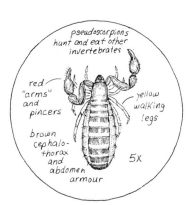

pseudoscorpions hunt and eat other invertebrates

red "arms" and pincers

yellow walking legs

brown cephalo-thorax and abdomen armour

5×

and whiter on the south side. If you walk around a trunk, you will find it subtly but definitely two-toned, as if it had a back and a belly. Aspen bark is not protected by a thick, corky dead layer, as are maple and oak. The living layer of the aspen tree is right at the surface, and it uses light to make plant food just as the leaves do. In winter, when the forest is bare and leafless, the sun shines full on the south sides of the aspen trunks, and they need the extra whiteness there to shield from and reflect the sun's rays. If the bark warmed and became active in winter sunshine, it would be killed by frost later.

As you step around bushes and between trees, the ground feels soft and moist. Shade and the leaf litter on the surface prevent evaporation. Also, below the shallow top layer of rich black chernozem lies a dense hardpan of clay, deposited long ago by glacial lakes, which prevents water from soaking through. The soil here is alkaline because of impeded drainage and the fact that, when moisture is brought to the surface by evaporation, minerals are brought up with it.

Step carefully, or your feet will crush one of the multitude of delicate fungi that take advantage

Helvella crispa

of the nutritious soil and moist, sheltered environment. Puffballs, always edible when young, spring up overnight after a drenching summer rain. Young mushrooms of the deadly *Amanita muscaria* look like little puffballs as they poke from the soft black earth. Each is encased in a thin white veil which breaks as the mushroom grows, leaving a telltale cup about the base of the stipe. This poisonous mushroom releases its spores from long, thin, radiating gills under its cap. The creamy-capped *Agaricus* mushroom, of which genus all seventy species are edible, also releases spores from long gills. Dark-gilled and rich-flavored *Coprinus*, the sensitive ink cap, grows in dense clusters above buried wood. *Russula*, with deep ivory gills and a lovely shiny cap which glows from pink to red, varies in edibility according to species. *Helvella crispa*, with its elegantly fluted stem, has no gills under its bunched, ruffled cap, but releases spores from a smooth undersurface. Brown, slimy-capped *Boletus*, edible but bland, has its entire cap filled with vertical tubes which release its

Amanita muscaria

spores, and appear as holes on the lower surface.

While looking for mushrooms you may discover a shiny gelatinous mass, bumpy and whitish on the outside, and soft, clear and jellylike inside. This is not something dead or cast off but a slime mold, which grows around stems and sticks, quite deliberately, of its own accord.

The exquisite moss, *Mnium*, its oval translucent leaves glistening along delicate strands of stem, hugs the moist bases of trees. If you lift a piece and examine it, more than the life of a plant is evident. Perhaps brisk ants with dark honey-colored abdomens and dark brown heads and thoraxes will immediately begin to worry for the safety of their young. Perhaps a pupated beetle larva, pure white with black eyes and only sculptural indications of the legs which will some day be useful, helplessly wriggles its pointed abdomen in discomfort at the bright light and dry air.

Everyone who has walked in the woods has found the path sometimes obstructed by clinging spider webs and long silken strands stretched between trees or spanning the space from one bush to another — spider roads to extra webs and choice sheltering places. Instead of blundering through webs with revulsion and impatience, become aware in a positive sense of the presence of spiders.

First you may notice the large, geometrically formed webs of the orb-weaving spiders, and stand fascinated by the startling beauty of the heavy-bodied arthropod herself. She has a round, firm, brightly patterned abdomen, and her thick, strong legs are poised close to the cephalothorax as she waits in the center of her web. Sometimes her mate is at the web, too, but harder to see. Male spiders are always smaller than females, especially among the orb weavers, whose females construct the webs. Her shiny silken masterpiece is hung with delicate gnats and midges, with softly feathered antennae, so fine as to look blurred. These small captives may be ignored by a well-fed spider, who will spring into action when the struggles of a larger insect shake the web. Then, quickly she runs to it, bites it to inject paralyzing venom, and deftly wraps it all around with silk.

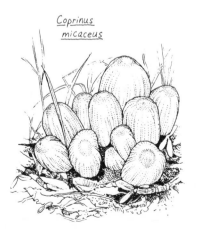

Coprinus micaceus

Once you have become interested in these lurking carnivores whose realm is the spaces between things, you will begin to see their handiwork everywhere you turn among the aspens. Just as vetch vines tangle about in the understory, winding curly thin tendrils tightly about the stems of their neighbors, some webs tangle among the sticks and stems. They make an inescapable

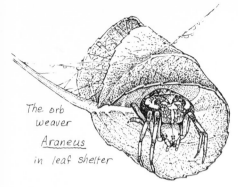

The orb
weaver
Araneus
in leaf shelter

trap for passing insects. In the thickest part of the maze, two or three leaves are twisted and tied together with strong strands that were pulled from the spinnerets of a cryptic little spider, now hiding in its homemade cave. Some webs are small, solid platforms, stretched tightly between twigs, reminding one of miniature trampolines. Very close to the ground, you will find evidence of spiders, where strands wind among the bases of bushes and the stiff stems of Fireweed. Some have made long tunnels and caves of silk in thick grassy places, and beneath the leaves of Dandelions.

Against the rough, corky lower bark of a big Cottonwood, a long-legged, slender-bodied spider, striped with yellow and brown, splays itself with legs forward and back to accentuate its linear effect against the bark. It will have one foreleg positioned watchfully on a fine thread running from the web to carry the impulses of any struggle which may occur there. Pluck a strand lightly and see if the spider runs along its tightwire to see what is caught in the trap. This doesn't always happen, but it is worth trying.

Spiders often retrace their steps, never really going far from the area to which they are accustomed. It is convenient for them to follow a thread of silk which they laid when they passed that way before. You can watch a spider pulling silk with a hind foot from the spinnerets at the tip of its abdomen, and attaching it as the foot steps, sometimes letting it pull out for a distance before attaching it again, and sometimes fastening it with each step as it walks.

If you look for spiders wherever you go, you will find them. Even while you are picking sweet purple and red Saskatoons in the pleasant dappled shade of the aspens, you will meet the delightful little spiders which peek out from within the bunches of berries, having trailed their delicate threads all around to make secure their little niche in the aspen grove.

Crab
Spider
on
Saskatoon
berries.

Prairie Wheat Farm

Man has made a different habitat of the prairie by his agricultural practises. This chapter is based mainly on a wheat farm near Brunkild, Manitoba.

Driving west from the spruce forests, *Sphagnum* bogs, and granite of the shield, or east out of the dusty, rolling cattle country of the western prairies, you find that the land is checkered with brown, green, and gold. The hills are gentle and, in some places, the land is so flat that the telephone poles merge evenly into straight dark ribbons along either side of the highway, which itself grows thinner and nearly disappears before it reaches the far horizon. When the early settlers crossed the plains the tallgrass prairie was an ocean of grass from horizon to horizon, the wind playing like a live thing, dimpling and rolling the wild grass for miles and miles, just as now you see it rippling vast fields of cultivated grasses: wheat, barley, oats, and rye. Now, only the railroad that brought the settlers west preserves the last remnants of tallgrass prairie along its right of way.

In pasture or tallgrass prairie, the insect population is as diverse as the flora, and the many grassland birds nest in the shelter of perennial grassy cover. But in the cultivated monotypic habitat of the grainfield

Richardson's Ground squirrel

which is harvested every fall and, in winter, lies stark and open to frost and snow, only the insect and fungus pests of grain can live, because there is nothing for any others to eat. Of birds, only the Horned Lark nests in the fields. It raises its brood quickly, feeding them with insects caught along the roads as the crop grows about the nest, and gleaning kernels from the stubble after harvest. When the

Wheat, a cultivated grass.

actual grain size.

icy winds of the prairie winter blow over the empty fields the Larks are far away in the southern plains and Mexico. In the more varied habitat along the roads, Western Meadowlarks sing on fence posts, watching over nests well hidden in bowers of roadside grass; young ground squirrels pop in and out of burrows, flicking tails, and wrestling and squealing; Killdeers incubate clutches of four speckled eggs on the flat, gravelly road shoulders; but only the Horned Larks, ground-nesting seed eaters, are adapted for life in a field of grain.

Wherever man establishes himself on the open prairie he plants windbreaks — narrow groves of trees along fencerows and all around his house and buildings, or just a single line of Cottonwoods, Manitoba maples, or willows if the ground is wet — across the path of the prevailing west wind. Thus he creates for himself a comfortable microclimate, shelter from the harshness of the sun and the relentless force of great masses of air, blowing unchecked from high pressure

areas to low pressure areas across the flat land. Storms can come quickly, looming purple-gray on the horizon, heavy clouds pushing toward you; you can smell the nearness of rain. The air grows alarmingly still and dark, and the leaves hang waiting. Robins, kingbirds, doves, orioles, Starlings, and Grackles fly to their nests to protect eggs and young as the first tentative drops spit from the sky. You can see the wind rushing like a herd of invisible bison, bending young wheat to the ground. When it reaches the windbreak, the trees seem to leap out of their stillness, swaying, tossing their branches, leaves all turning silver backsides. The lashing boughs of aspen and Cottonwood hiss and scintillate as their leaves flutter and rattle. Rain streams down in sheets and water pours from the gutters of the roofs. The soil has turned from gray to black and puddles form where a few moments ago it was cracked and dry.

Sometimes, instead of lifegiving rain, the storm brings hail, hurling tons of hard ice to the earth, breaking stems, cutting off ripening heads of grain, chopping wheat into acres of worthless grass clippings. Imagine the sight of green crops turned into ploughed fields by the force of hail! Wet years occur, when low areas flood and must be reseeded, or the soil remains too soft and wet to bear planting machinery. Dry years come too, when soil is blown for miles, filling in ditches and settling out of the air inside houses and barns. Seed is scattered, exposed on the roads, and drifted into ditches with the dust.

But now it is raining. The face of the storm has passed and steady drops fall from a dull, white sky. Robins and Brewer's Blackbirds search for worms on the fresh, bright grass of the lawn, and doves mince across the gravel by the barn. Kingbirds flash from tree to tree, calling and checking their territories for intruders, and swoop suddenly from leafy perches after passing flies and flying beetles. Insects are on the move, out of hastily taken shelter, and birds are hunting them, eager to find and eat those that were knocked down and wet by the rain. Barn Swallows are fly-catching, lacing the space above the barnyard in an aerial ballet, their rusty breasts glowing within silhouettes of narrow wings and forked tails.

Many bird species make use of the planted windbreaks of the prairie farms, returning every year to the trees that they know to nest and raise their young. Black and orange orioles meticulously weave swinging nests high in the trees. Several pairs of Robins construct twiggy nests close to the trunks of Apple and Box Elder, as do kingbirds. They arrive from the south later than the Robins, and sometimes a Robin may find its eggs on the ground and its nest occupied by a pair of kingbirds, even more aggressive than themselves, and willing to fight anything with wing, beak, and claw.

The yodelling coo of Mourning Doves sounds soft in the evening from fir boughs and barn lofts. These subtly iridescent dawn-beige birds build very flimsy nests. The best way to view the eggs is from beneath, through spaces in the nest. Often an egg or two will roll out, when the dove flushes in a whirr at someone's approach. Doves cannot

Wild Oats
Danthonia intermedia

The seeds work far down
into damp soil
by untwisting the spike, or awn,
and can remain dormant
for several years
before sprouting.

Wild Oats competes
for water and light
with cultivated grain,
and is very difficult
to eradicate.

defend their nests, so, if a nest is slight, perhaps it is less noticeable to egg predators. Doves make pigeon's milk in their crops, which enriches regurgitated food with protein, and makes it possible to raise three or four broods a year.

While I was in a tangled willow windbreak beside a dugout pond, a pair of Robins was very disturbed, hopping about from branch to branch above me. They squeaked sharply and constantly, "Peerp, peerp, peerp, peerp, peerp, peerp, peerp," with head feathers raised, rusty breasts fluffed, and eyes blinking in indignation. Then I found the nest, only a meter above the ground, where a nearly fledged young Robin hunched, still, watching me. The racket of its parents' scolding made me feel uneasy. A chalky-breasted Eastern Kingbird made his hostile appearance, with tiny scarlet crest lifted. Drawn by the commotion, a male Redwinged Blackbird, trilling fiercely, and a vivid black and orange Baltimore Oriole, were ready to mob. Predator discouragement is a community effort. Chastened, I left, flushing another young Robin into clumsy flight from a nearby branch.

House sparrows appreciate farm buildings, clustering around spilled grain like flies, and nesting under eaves and behind gutter pipes. In the spring, House Wrens pop in and out of any hole that is just the right size, searching for nesting places, sometimes getting trapped in the house. Barn swallows cheep and chatter as they build sturdy nests of mud balls, with bits of string and feathers for extra strength, on rafters and under ledges, and especially inside, if there is always a way in and out. They often renovate the same nest year after year, and become accustomed to the presence and noise of people and machinery, coming and going about the tasks of the wheat farm.

On the open prairie, the scattered groups of planted trees are oases for migrating birds in spring and fall. Then you may see Red-eyed Vireos, Swainson's Thrushes, Yellow Warblers, Redstarts, and Song Sparrows from the aspen parkland; Juncos, White-throated sparrows, Red-breasted Nuthatches, and Myrtle Warblers from the boreal forest; and Black-poll Warblers, and White-crowned and Harris sparrows from the edge of the tundra.

Every night the barn swallows take the same positions, female on the nest and male perched close beside. Brunkild, Man. 14 June 1977

The farm is shared by much more than birds. A family of skunks may have lived for several generations under an old granary, and earned the respect of many farm dogs. The white stripes of the skunks' long soft coats gleam in the darkness as they nose their nocturnal way across the dewy lawn, hunting earthworms and, after spring rains, Tiger Salamanders, and snuffling under old logs and boards in the windbreak for beetles and grubs. The mask-faced Raccoon, who sleeps in the great hollow trunk of the oldest willow, catches frogs in the grass, feels for crayfish at the muddy edge of the dugout, and raids the garden by night for ripe sweet corn. The ever present voles live their mouse-lives in the grassy margins of the windbreaks, and in fallow fields. They are prey for Red-tailed Hawks and Harriers in summer, and Rough-legged Hawks and Snowy Owls in winter. Large-eyed Deer Mice, with immaculately white feet and bellies, skitter secretly through their trails and tunnels, more secure in the shelter of trees or buildings. A shy Red Fox, whose den is somewhere out of sight where the ground is well drained, hunts mice and ground squirrels in the morning and evening.

Some farms have rectangular dugouts, made for domestic water supply, or for livestock. You will find the banks pelted with dark green sedge, starred with yellow buttercups, lined with tall cattails, and leaping with Leopard Frogs. Burrowing crayfish may lurk in its muddy bottom, and each year it is a nursery for Mallards or teal.

this young Robin sits very still, trying to escape notice, because it can't fly well yet.

American
Avocets

Marbled Godwit

Prairie Slough

The profusion of small lakes and ponds in the northern prairies results from the irregular way in which retreating glaciers have affected the landscape, ploughing up dams of soil and broken rock, and leaving big chunks of ice in the surface to melt into bodies of water. This chapter is based on the western end of Grassy Lake, Alberta, and many other sloughs in the southern part of Alberta, Saskatchewan, and Manitoba.

The highest concentration of prairie life occurs at the slough. Many species of shorebirds nest on the banks and gather food from water teeming with invertebrates. In the spring the great shorebirds seek you out and circle around you; chestnut-winged Marbled Godwits, black and white Avocets and Willets, and buffy Long-Billed Curlews. Their nests are simple exposed dimples in the soil, and their only defense is distraction, filling the senses of the intruder by a continual display of plumage and raucous sound in an attempt to attract attention from their eggs or young. It is pathetic to watch a female Avocet try to lure you away from her nest, struggling, flopping, and uttering hurt cries until you are sure she must die soon; and it is exhilarating to be nearly brushed by the wingtips of a curlew, circling as it calls "Curlee, Curlee, Curlee?". The curlew's thin, downcurved, blunt-tipped bill is longer than its body, and its feathers are rusty colored and finely patterned like a rich tweed. A Killdeer, with high white forehead and chest boldly banded with black, flutters away, uttering piercing cries, "Tiook, tiook, tiook." Her buffy wing and orange tail drag as if broken, and her elusive chicks scatter in all directions. Ring-billed Gulls wheel and scream, for they too have their eggs in exposed nests somewhere near.

The small hummocks of grass that you see, surrounded by water, may bear the Franklin's Gull's eggs. Little Wilson's Phalaropes, with a tinge of rust on their sides, and skunk-striped heads, circle close above, uttering "Rent, rent, rent," softly, like a distant quacking of ducks. While you stand in sight there will be a constant commotion of many birds. Some dip and preen nonchalantly, hoping that you will approach them rather than search for their eggs or young. All are very concerned, and they all know how close you are to their nests. There may be dozens of pairs of birds nesting at a slough, but the nests themselves are hard to see. A search for hidden eggs may disclose those of a meadowlark, white, brown-flecked, and the size of Robin's eggs, in a cave of arched grass. At the slough edge, the damp mud is pocked with cattle and antelope tracks and powdered with minerals where the alkali water evaporates. There, Avocet eggs, olive with black splashes, are grouped in a slight

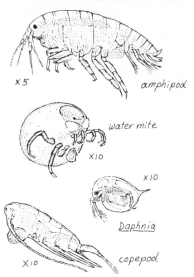

x5   amphipod

water mite

x10

x10

Daphnia

x10   copepod

Small arthropods of sloughs and ditches. West end of Grassy Lake, Alta. 7 June 1977

hollow on top of a knoll, the short-leaved grass trailing around them all rimed with white salt. Exposed though it is, the nest is invisible until you are quite close, so be careful not to crush the eggs as you walk.

The eastern prairie receives more rainfall than the west, and its potholes are lined with cattails aswarm with blackbirds and teeming with ducks of all kinds; but because of the low rainfall and drastic fluctuation of water level, the banks of the sloughs in the western prairies are open, abounding with shorebirds. The gentle hills that flank a slough in cattle country are often dotted with bushes of wild rose, and prickly cacti crouch in the coarse grass. Pussytoes, *Antenaria*, with clusters of dryish, fuzzy, white flower heads on short stems, are abundant. Here, on high

Tiny *Pseudacris*, newly trans- formed from tadpoles climb out of the water onto the vegetation in June.

They absorb the last of their tails and turn from vegetarians to carnivores.

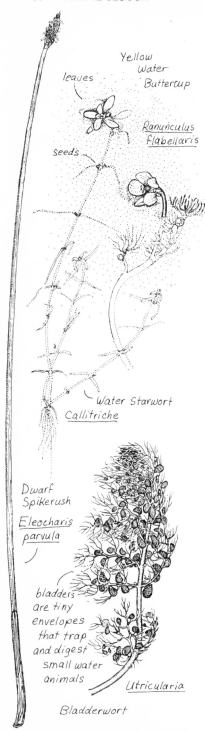

Yellow
Water
Buttercup

leaves

*Ranunculus
Flabellaris*

seeds

Water Starwort
Callitriche

Dwarf
Spikerush

*Eleocharis
parvula*

bladders
are tiny
envelopes
that trap
and digest
small water
animals

Utricularia

Bladderwort

ground, male Chestnut-sided Longspurs run about, hunting insects between display flights. These handsome little birds with dark heads and chestnut sides have flashy white tails with central black wedges which they flaunt at their neighbors, singing in long, fluttering downward flights. Their tails are spread and they sing bits of song even as they hunt for food on the ground, nervously keeping an eye on their territorial neighbors.

Below the short, salt-encrusted grass at the slough edge, Water Buttercups with wet strings of foliage hold glimmering, white-petalled flowers just above the surface. Bladderwort raises single yellow snapdragonlike flowers high on long stalks. In low-banked ends of sloughs where the water level is relatively stable, a stand of cattails may survive droughts, and flat-bladed *Carex* stands even in height, yellow-green tips bending softly in a little breeze. Tall *Scirpus*, with hollow green stems and frowzy clusters of tan flowers where the stem narrows near the tip, reflect themselves in still water.

Electric blue dragonflies poise weightlessly on a bladderwort flower. They fly in tandem, the male holding the tail tip of the female, and they both hover gracefully as she dips her ovipositor to the water surface here and there, dropping the eggs that will produce another generation of their kind. Pale blue butterflies, with fine black spots on their fringed wings, scintillate from cow-turned clod to buttercup to sedge stem, and a black, semiaquatic spider, whose body hairs repel water, scurries over wet mud. A Yellow-headed Blackbird, enthroned on a marsh-bound Tumbleweed, is feathered like black velvet with a buttercup yellow hood. He challenges, "Took, alook, alook, duck, duck, blee!" and the Red-winged Blackbirds are careful not to trespass. Poised above its rippled image in the water, a Black Tern hovers against the wind, long pointed wings flopping rhythmically, and chants, "Ick, ick, ick, ick." Little dark Coots, their rounded backs low in the water, dot the reflection of the wide prairie sky.

The reflection breaks, undulating in long ripples, as the head and back of a Muskrat cruise from the bank into the middle of the slough, pause for a moment, and then go down, head first. Sneak quietly closer to the Muskrat's burrow in the bank before it comes back with the green grassy water plants, Western Ditchgrass, trailing from the sides of its mouth, its small dark eyes glinting. Brushing against the margin of the floating algae, the Muskrat makes a quick turn where the algae parts and, after shaking like a dog, sits and preens before eating a little of its harvest. As its black paws brush over the thick fur, long wet guard hairs part to show fluffy underfur that stays dry even under water. A godwit flies overhead, screaming as he sees you settle yourself more comfortably on the prickly sedges behind the Muskrat's back. The little animal instantly takes note of the alarm call and freezes perfectly still, not even taking the plant stem out of its mouth, waiting

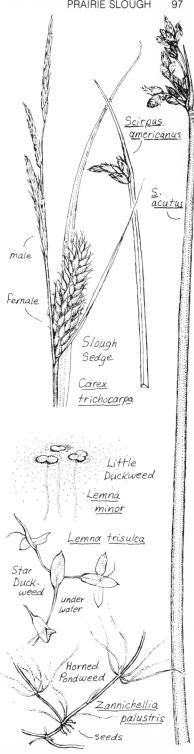

Scirpus americanus

S. acutus

male

female

Slough Sedge

Carex trichocarpa

Little Duckweed

Lemna minor

Lemna trisulca

Star Duckweed

under water

Horned Pondweed

Zannichellia palustris

seeds

for the danger to pass. Later it eats the tender bases of the weed and, heading out for more, it dives again. The shiny black, nearly hairless tail whips about, like a fighting snake, at the surface. Burdened with green streamers, the Muskrat comes straight back toward you and dives beneath the bank. After a few minutes, a gurgling sound comes from the hole about a meter up the bank from the entrance as the Muskrat moves from the air-filled den down through the water-filled tunnel on its way out for more. If the den needs bedding material, the Muskrat works with hands and teeth, quickly cutting sedges in mid-stem. Short butts sticking out of one side, and long tips out of the other, it packs in as many sedges as will fit between its cheeks and its orange-colored chisel-sharp front teeth. These teeth are constantly growing, and they sharpen as they work against one another, like the teeth of the Beaver. Down the Muskrat goes into the burrow with its bedding; and this time it stays there.

As you straighten yourself, a pair of Avocets take to the air. They had been quietly walking in the shallows on long, pale blue legs, swishing their long, curved bills sideways through the water, feeding. Round and round the slough they fly, squeaking their annoyance and concern. One lands on the far side of the slough. Its elegant rusty-buff neck is held straight and the black, upturned bill shows sharply against the salt-rimed slough bank as it turns its smooth, pale head, eyeing you suspiciously.

In the water, frantic gray and white water bugs with big black eyes dash about over the mud-filmed algae tangle, and writhing ivory worms poke from the brown mud. Brilliant *Cyclops*, with two orange oars at the head, and one blood-red eye, row jerkily here and there. Ostracods roll through the water, their swimming legs waving from the crack between clamlike valves. Big, dull-red water mites barrel through a weedy obstacle course like animated satin cushions with dimples of interior muscle attachments to flatten and streamline the shape of their bodies. Eight tiny legs propel them, briskly thrashing away like egg beaters.

The snail *Lymnaea stagnalis* glides into view around the edge of a sodden, brown cattail leaf. The snail's soft, gray body is nearly transparent, but strong, as it lifts its tall, spired shell of satiny dark amber and tilts the aperture to the surface. The flat, faintly ripply underside of its foot meets the air and then the water is opened with a faint pop by the mantle rim, curled into a funnel at the margin of the shell. By muscular movements of the mantle floor, the snail exchanges stale air for fresh. A constantly moving, finely ciliated surface, glistening with microscopic hairs, ensures that no water enters into the dark interior of the snail. The hole in the water disappears when the thin mantle edge is drawn tight and slips back under the shell. Sometimes the gray foot continues to slide up, and rides the surface like a raft, turning this way and that, with its margin cupped, just a little, to repel water. In rhythmic licks, the round mouth collects the thin surface scum of the water. Then the mouth dips under and the rest follows as it crawls ghostily down the green-slimed stem of cattail, scraping algae with its cat's-tongue radula. Microscopic examination of these tiny hooked teeth is often necessary to identify

species of snails whose shells are similar. Aquatic snails produce lumps of jelly containing clear, round golden eggs, stuck to underwater vegetation. Look very closely at every detail in the water before you, and scoop some of the bottom up in a dip net to see if you can find other, smaller kinds of snail than *Lymnaea stagnalis*. Notice the wealth of all forms of invertebrate life, each adapted in its own way to a place in the prairie slough.

Little water striders skate on the shining surface, not wet at all, hunting for mites and springtails. Flies with metallic, yellow-green thoraxes and long, narrow wings folded over their backs jump one another on the bank and on floating vegetation.

One hop propels *Rana pipiens*, the Leopard Frog, from underfoot into the water, where it sits low, still as a statue and green as the grass, with two yellow stripes, and black spots like the shadows among the delicate plants on the bottom. Leopard Frogs avoid the feet of large animals, and sunbathe on cool mornings in the quickly sun-warmed water held by footprints in the mud. When startled, they propel themselves nose first toward the water's dark deepness, with arms pinned to their sides, and strong legs held straight together between thrusts, disappearing quickly in the soft silty bottom.

The Chorus Frog, *Pseudacris*, "griks" from the bank, and quiets as you approach. Pintail ducks burst from the sedge-grown shallow end of the slough with a rush of splashes, and fly straight away with necks outstretched and a blur of wings, quacking hoarsely. Then a pair of Mallards churns noisily from water to air, white tails spread like fans and iridescent green necks reaching for clearance. The blue patches of a teal's wings match the sky as she circles, watching you leave; then she drops by her nest on the far side of the slough.

Sagebrush Desert

Desert occurs naturally in the extreme rainshadow of the western mountains.
Here, low rainfall and high temperatures make the soil so dry that plants must
compete for moisture underground more than for light above the surface. The
plant cover is incomplete and the soil is exposed. In the grasslands of partial rain
shadow regions, desert is created by overgrazing and careless cultivation
methods. Water is lost in runoff, and topsoil is removed by wind and water erosion.
Eventually only plants which are able to live in desert conditions can survive. This
chapter is based on some of the few flat tracts of natural desert in Canada, which
are not irrigated, in the Similkameen and Okanagan river valleys in southern
British Columbia.

One of the best ways of seeing desert life is with the eyes of one who
lives there. Let me introduce you to a small jumping spider who is soft
and velvety, cream-colored with neat brown stripes, with a pair of big
shiny black eyes, more powerful than the eyes of anything else her size.
She is a hunter and lives by her eyes. You will notice her by the short little
runs she makes, and how she stops and tilts her cephalothorax to see
what big thing has come. She is hungry, and won't remain distracted for

long. As soon as she is satisfied that you are not chasing her or trying to squash her she will resume her hunting, and you may lean very close to watch.

See how neatly her thick, smoothly-furred legs are tucked around her, making her look more like a weevil than like the splay-legged gray-striped running spider which also hunts here. She keeps her legs bunched up, always ready to jump should she see a little movement. She pivots impatiently this way and that on the summit of a small lump of dry dust, looking for what? Suddenly she stares upward, rubs her white pedipalps against one another excitedly as a minute blurr of wings, perhaps a gnat, circles and is gone. Two bright reflections of the sun flash from her midnight eyes as she holds her position for a moment to see if the little fly will land on the stiff round grass stems just above. You will begin to be impatient too, and try to see what she is looking at as she turns this way and that, twisting her body to stare here and there. A black and red ant scrambles busily across the nearest mound of sand, kept clear and trampled by all its relatives, and the spider snaps about to face it alertly. An ant walks by a few centimeters from her and, when the nearsighted animal is close enough to see her, quick as a wink, she turns her back on it — perhaps to signal that she is not hunting it. Ants are very fierce and, besides, they taste strongly of formic acid. There are many ants scurrying about here and there, going in and out of holes, carrying dead things, or gently twiddling antennae with each other. The spider is distracted whenever one comes near but she never threatens or jumps. There are other things that she looks for. Now you see them. Very tiny bright orange, glossy mites, with many legs, dart about, in and out of the holes of the ant nest, and in and out of the shade of lumps and nobs of dust. They are nearly as fast as the spider. There! She sees one, fully fifteen centimeters away, and in an instant she is off her viewpoint and across the rugged terrain to where she had seen its movement. She rummages around the vicinity. Can't find it. It is hiding in a shallow crack, very still. The spider moves to a high spot close by and peers down and around. When the mite moves again, she spots it instantly; she shuffles her legs nervously, the way a cat wiggles before leaping, and pounces. While the mite is being adjusted beneath her pedipalps and its juices consumed, the spider is alert and looking for more. The tidbit finished, she moves tentatively away, waving her forelegs up and down as if testing the air, sees a mite on the bare side of the ant hill and darts after it as the orange speck dodges here and there. Missed! It's a hard life. Like most animals in the desert, the spider doesn't drink water. It gets its only moisture from the morsels it can catch. On a hot sunny day you can understand how the spider is hunting for its very life.

Jumping spider *Pellenes*, adult female.
5x size. Similkameen River valley,
14.5 km W of Osoyoos, B.C. 29 May
1977

As you wait with the hunting spider for something to move within her small world, in your broader world of vision many things are moving. Black and tan striped beetles, only as large as the head of a pin, crawl about over thin dusty mats of stiff moss and the rough gray twisted stems of sage, and tiny white leaf hoppers spring from silvery sagebrush leaves to feathery Yarrow. A black tenebrionid beetle with short antennae and finely textured back walks closely around the base of a sage bush, careful to stay in the shade. This is the hot part of the day, and he is black. If they are not colored like the soil, to be invisible to predators or prey, desert animals are either black or white. White, to stay active in the sun for more of the day, reflecting the light and heat; and black to warm up more quickly when the sun first dispels the chill of the clear desert night. Melanin, the pigment which produces a black color, also lends greater strength to the exoskeleton, and makes it more waterproof. Any living being, plant or animal, which consumes very little moisture, must guard against evaporation. Prickly pear cacti, *Opuntia*, do this with a

Two parasites of sagebrush. Similkameen River valley, B.C. 30 May 1977

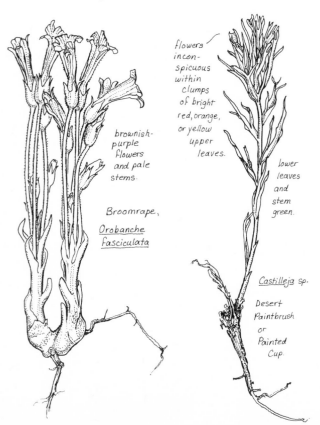

flowers incon-
spicuous
within
clumps
of bright
red, orange,
or yellow
upper
leaves.

brownish-
purple
flowers
and pale
stems.

lower
leaves
and
stem
green.

Broomrape,

*Orobanche
fasciculata*

Castilleja sp.

Desert
Paintbrush
or
Painted
Cup.

waxy cuticle, smooth and firm on their fat, green stem lobes. They open their breathing pores, or stomata, only at night, when evaporation is slower.

The *Opuntia* uses its stem both for water storage and photosynthesis. Its leaves have been modified to long white spines, which discourage grazing beasts from munching them, and also aid in the dispersal of the species by sticking into feet, since sections of the stem can take root after they are kicked off. The leaves of most desert plants are

Twig of Tumbleweed, *Salsola kali*. Similkameen River valley, B.C. 29 May 1977

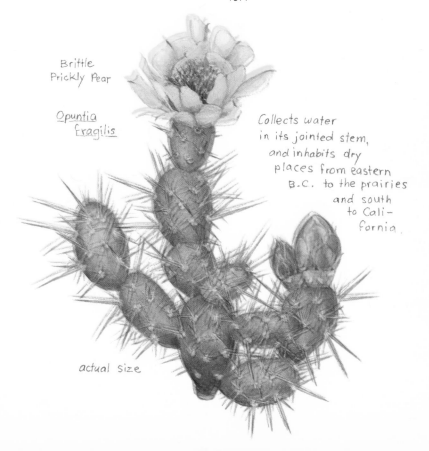

Brittle Prickly Pear

Opuntia fragilis

Collects water in its jointed stem, and inhabits dry places from eastern B.C. to the prairies and south to California.

actual size

narrow, and seem to be either flat and fuzzy or thick and smooth. The flat, whitely fuzzy surfaces help to retain the humidity of the leaf and also reflect the hot sunlight. Those which aren't fuzzy are as near to round as can be managed, presenting a minimum surface to the dry air.

The leaves of Bitterroot poke from the soil, shining, firm, and round in bunches like swollen fir needles. Rock Cress, with a bunch of small four-petalled white flowers at its top, appears to have both of the desert leaf forms. Its thick clump of small basal leaves and the few tiny leaves hugging its tall stem are flat and lightly furred. The solid, smooth seed pods which hang down along the stem as each flower matures, look like leaves, and aid in photosynthesis. Daggerpod nestles in the thin, round-bladed grass. Its spade-shaped leaves are silvered with soft, fine white hairs, like the leaves of the spicy sagebrush.

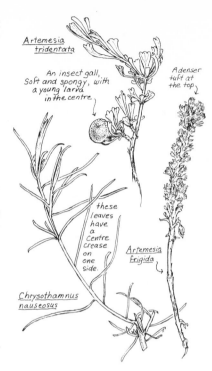

Artemesia tridentata

An insect gall, soft and spongy, with a young larva in the centre

A denser tuft at the top

these leaves have a centre crease on one side.

Artemesia frigida

Chrysothamnus nauseosus

Three kinds of sagebrush. E of Osoyoos, B.C. 30 May 1977

The chemicals in sagebrush are poisonous to most animals, and those that graze sage eat sparingly, mixing it with other plants. Sagebrush is also the reason for the few species of plants here, as the decay of its fallen leaves releases toxic compounds into the soil, limiting the growth of many plants that would compete. The spicy scent of its defense fills the air as you brush its foliage. From near the ground, the sage bushes look like stunted, twisted trees, their gray bark encrusting the gnarled trunks with vertical shreds. Sagebrush, being wind-pollinated, raises, from the ends of its branches, long thin flower stalks, which in spring bear only chaffy bits and whisps of last summer's flowers. The rest of the bush is low and contorted, often hugging the ground, providing shade for desert creatures.

Grasshoppers are loth to leave the midday shade. They move from branch to branch as

The roots of Bitterroot can survive extreme dehydration, but the large, fragile pink flowers bloom near the ground, shaded by grasses, in May, before the hot summer months.

A black Tenebrionid beetle stays in the shade.

you pass close by a bush. Meadowlarks, Magpies, and Racer snakes hunt its kind by sight, so the grasshopper is speckled black and white, as nearly invisible as can be. You will see only a movement in the leaves or grass, until it flies, when for a few moments it is like a flickering orange flame or a lilting, clattering butterfly. Then it disappears, closing brilliant wings and dropping into anonymity among the silvery sage. It has fooled many birds by this behavior, which doubles as a mating display.

Pronghorn Antelope, *Antilocapra americana*, browse on sagebrush.

In the spaces between dry clumps of desert grass, much of what seems like bare, cracked dust is instead patches of crusty gray lichen, crisscrossed by a network of thin cracks like a sunbacked scum of sandy mud. Its identity is revealed by little dark gray-lined holes for the production and release of its spores. You can walk over these lichens and the slight, tightly packed mounds of dense, brittle desert moss, without guessing that there is anything living there on the parched earth.

Many laboratory experiments have shown that desert organisms cannot survive for long in the high temperatures that occur in their habitat; but you can see that, if left to their own devices, they are just as comfortable as the plants and animals of any other habitat. The pocket

Racer, *Coluber constrictor*, hunting Great Basin Pocket Mouse, *Perognathus parvus*. Similkameen River valley, B.C. 29 May 1977

mouse comes out at night to harvest seeds, and closes his tunnels behind him in the morning. You may happen upon a number of shallow dimples in an area of soft dust, a favorite dust bathing site for one of these silky-furred solitary rodents.

Spadefoot toads spend most of their lives sleeping at the bottoms of long burrows, down in the desert earth, their baby-soft skins able to soak up the least bit of moisture. They climb to the mouth of the burrow at night to catch nocturnal insects and, at the signal of a few drops of rain, begin to travel. When a sudden spring or summer rain fills temporary ponds spadefoots aggregate in vast numbers to call and breed. In a race with drying puddles, their eggs soon hatch into swarms of tadpoles, which, if the water level drops dangerously low, will eat each other. Even so, all die if the water disappears before their growth is finished. Only weeks after spawning, the survivors have transformed into gray-green, pug-nosed toads with large eyes, and stiff black spurs on their heels — spades for burrowing backwards down to moisture beneath the warm dry surface where you walk.

Tumbleweed grows in the late summer, when other plants are dormant, and when there is little competition for what water is left in the soil. Then, it is green-stemmed, with prickles for leaves, and at the base of each one nestles a small flower, with petals like pink tissue; now, however, the Tumbleweed is dry and yellow. Many bushes are uprooted — light prickly baskets dispersing their seed as the wind tumbles them far from home. Once a female Horned Lark was alarmed by a Tumbleweed blowing over her nest under an arch of grass. She flew up, startled, right into the bush; then the Tumbleweed continued its journey, while the bird remained trapped in its thorny cage.

The White-Tailed Jackrabbit, sitting in the shade of a sage bush, radiates his body heat into the sky from the surfaces of his large ears, his nose twitching and his brown eyes alert for coyotes. Pink stars of *Phlox* bloom in delicate profusion in the season of occasional rain, and white and yellow asters nod on long sparsely-leaved stems. All tell their portion of the beauty of the desert, and how it is home for those who know how to live there.

Spadefoot toad, *Scaphiopus intermontanus*. Osoyoos, B.C. 30 May 1977

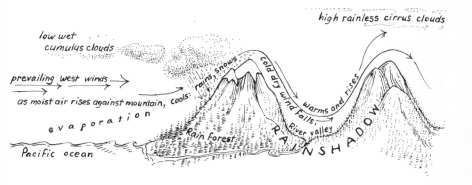

- high rainless cirrus clouds
- low wet cumulus clouds
- prevailing west winds
- as moist air rises against mountain, cools
- evaporation
- Pacific ocean
- rains, snows
- cold dry wind falls, warms and rises
- Rain forest
- River valley
- RAINSHADOW

Rainshadow Forest

The inland peaks and valleys of the Cordillera are all in rainshadow; forests dominated by Ponderosa Pine extend from southern British Columbia to California. This chapter is based on the Fraser Valley, especially 42 km south of Lillooet, and Chilliwack Lake, British Columbia.

The slope is steep under the tall Ponderosa Pines. In the hot light shade cast by long thin needles, two kinds of grasses strike the eye, a tall kind and a short kind, both with long narrow seed heads and thin leaves. This sparse vegetation is yellow in late summer; it grew up, flowered, and went to seed early in the season while there was moisture in the ground.

Here and there, close to the ground, are touches of green. Yarrow, with soft feathery leaves, raises a flat cluster of composite flowers on a tall, lightly furred stem. Pinch the tip from one of the tender leaves. Crush it, and breathe the air filled with sharp, tangy fragrance. Yarrow can be used as an astringent, as an anaesthetic for wounds, and as a diuretic tea, good for the bladder and kidneys. Green also are the little flat mats of Pussytoes, *Antenaria*. When moisture is no longer available to sustain their flat form and fresh color, the finely fuzzy whorls of pale green, sharp-tipped leaves curl up in close, white, lichenlike clusters. Whispers of green also occur among dense tan scraggles of *Selaginella densa*. Much coarser and more protective of its moisture than some related wet-living species, its branches of tightly fitting leaves arch up with faintly colored tips from the crisp, pale body of its mat.

Sheltered by close groups of pines, rusty brown needles and flaked pine bark lie thick and slippery on the soil, letting a few slim grasses through; but, in places, nothing can manage to keep the soil from slipping with the rain and blowing with the wind. Small patches of grasses grasp it with fine tangled roots, and tree roots stretch across under its surface; but the soil escapes where fire has damaged the vegetation or floods have cut gullies and draws. Often, where minor erosion has set in, the spring thaw and rains cause a landslide, leaving the mountainside sliced as clean as if it were cut with a knife. On slopes so steep that no soil can form, slides are vast areas of broken rock. You may see the tiny form of a large Black Bear making infinitesimal progress with large strides up an exceedingly steep scree. The rocks and boulders that he dislodges roll down until they reach the forest below.

In the hot, dry breeze between yourself and the distant climbing bear, *Polistes*, a paper wasp, flies on narrow brown wings with long yellow legs trailing, to find some soft wood and shred it into the paper pulp which it uses to enlarge its nest. The valley echoes with loud, hoarse bird voices as strong-winged gray, black, and white Nutcrackers with their crops full of sweet unhulled pine nuts swoop and circle to light atop pines across the valley. They will store these nuts for the winter, but remove shells from those that they regurgitate to feed their noisy young. In the dry heat the scales of the pine cones stretch open wide, and silky-winged seeds whirl through the air. Pulled down by the weight of their rough, speckle-shelled nuts and held back by their papery wings, they are tossed aloft by rising air and turbulent wind. The Nutcrackers pick up the fallen seeds on the ground or wrench them out of the unopened cones in the trees.

This forest favors nuthatches, and three species hammer open pine nuts and glean insects from the tree trunks and branches. "Ank, ank," sounds the Red-breasted Nuthatch. You can see its white eye stripe as it cocks its head watchfully. The Pigmy Nuthatch with a gray-brown cap, and without a white eye stripe, calls "Pip, pip." It lives only in Ponderosa Pine forest. A larger White-breasted Nuthatch, head down on a pine trunk, cries nasally "quank, quank, quank."

Beetles and ants walk about in the grass and among the pine needles, but no creature lives here who must drink water, except those who can fly or walk a long distance for it. Spill water that *you* have carried

Selaginella densa

here, though, and flies and wasps will smell it and come to drink from the mud. Notice that there are no mice scuttling through the grass or squeaking in the evening here. No squirrels chatter and chirr from branches overhead, and no chipmunks scamper up tree trunks, stripes flashing. There are no skunks to snuffle under logs at night, foraging with soft, black hands, and no marmot holes, or dens of fierce, stripe-faced Badgers. There are no molehills or tunnels to soften the earth, and not even earthworms. The soil is sandy and dry. Tender black crickets and pale, dusty grasshoppers have very dry droppings, and lose almost no water through their skins. They survive on water produced by their bodies from

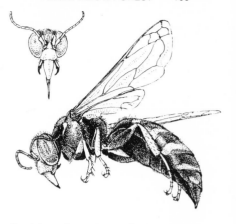

Bembix, a digger wasp, digs burrows in dry sandy places and catches flying insects. Wapiti River S of Grand Prairie, Alta., 11 August 1976

seeds and dry plants. During the day, crickets rove and harvest, waving sensitive antennae at the world around them. In the evening, the mountain shadows climb the western slopes, the air cools and grows still, the moon sets, and stars glow brightly; then, the crickets sing. There may be brief cloud cover by morning, but not for long, as the air blows warm from sunlit valleys. There is little rain or moisture for these mountains.

When it does rain, the steep slopes and poorly developed soils allow most of the water to run off or go down into the gravelly subsoil. Later, groundwater appears, cold and pure, in little streams coursing down gullies once cut by spring meltwater from the peaks. Precious water cascades in thin silver lines over precipices, leaps and boils and roars through jagged rocky chasms, tumbling and grinding angular rocks into smooth ones, and depositing gravel bars where the river widens on the valley floor. There, the tall Douglas Fir and Western Red Cedar stand, and a thin green line of undergrowth perches back from the broad rock-grinding zone of spring floods.

The mammal life of the rainshadow forest is concentrated near water. The impatient Chickaree, a western Red Squirrel with a gray-brown back and tail and a foxy belly, peeks and flirts around the great buttressed bases of the stringy-barked cedars, and scolds in familiar *Tamiasciurus* fashion. It is soon out of sight and busy harvesting fir cones, which thump to the ground nearby.

Here, the Chickaree, leaning down from branches and logs to drink of the stream's icy wetness, has all the water it needs. So does the largest of meadow mice *Microtus richardsoni*, who scurries along its well

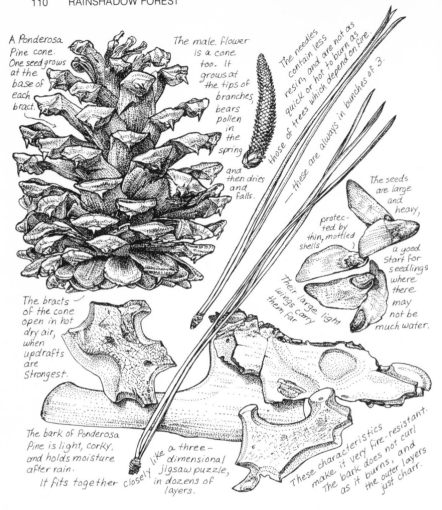

A Ponderosa Pine cone. One seed grows at the base of each bract.

The male flower is a cone too. It grows at the tips of branches, bears pollen in the spring and then dries and falls.

The needles contain less resin, and are not as quick or hot to burn as those of trees which depend on fire.

— these are always in bunches of 3.

The seeds are large and heavy, protected by thin, mottled shells, a good start for seedlings where there may not be much water.

Their large light wings carry them far

The bracts of the cone open in hot dry air, when updrafts are strongest.

The bark of Ponderosa Pine is light, corky, and holds moisture after rain. It fits together closely like a three-dimensional jigsaw puzzle, in dozens of layers.

These characteristics make it very fire-resistant. The bark does not curl as it burns, and the outer layers just char.

There is not enough water in the rainshadow for Ponderosa Pines to grow close together. Plenty of light reaches the forest floor, and the mature trees do not need to burn down to open the canopy for seedlings. They have adapted well to survive fires, and grow tall to give the wind their seed. Fraser River valley, 42 km S of Lilloet, B.C. 1 September 1976

worn, secret paths among the Vine Maple, mint and Fireweed to drink where water has pooled against an old fallen tree. This rodent has the same shape and fur texture as the much smaller common Meadow Vole, *Microtus pennsylvanicus* but is fifteen centimeters of fat, brown, gray-bellied body with a short, bicolored tail.

While glancing along the stream bank in search of giant meadow mouse burrows, some of which open underwater, your eye may be caught by the short curtseying bobs of a fat, slate-gray bird with small

wings and a short, raised tail. Its body is the shape of a drop of water, and it pipes a sharp "Zeet" call that sounds well against the many notes of the rushing stream. You will be astonished, as I have been, to see the bird which had been standing, bobbing, on a rock in midstream, pop right into the water and stay under as if it belonged there. If you are near, you may see it scooting about over the stones on the bottom, probing beneath them with its slender bill, and darting after minnows. Dippers find flat mayfly and stone fly nymphs hugging the rocks underwater, long, grublike alderfly larvae, caddisworms in their cases, and young midges and blackflies bound to the bottom with silk. They also eat the tadpoles of *Ascaphus*, the Tailed Frog, which have huge suction-cup mouths, and, in season, Dippers eat berrylike orange-pink, salmon eggs. The Dipper pops out of the water right in front of you, its feathers dry as dry, curtseys rapidly once or twice on a stone,

Male flowers of Ponderosa Pine. 10.5 km SSW of Princeton, B.C. 28 May 1977

Dipper, *Cinclus mexicanus*. Notice the
slim probing bill, and the thick pads
under the strong, flexible toes.
Paleface Creek, near Chilliwack Lake,
B.C. 17 September 1976

and then becomes a fishlike flicker down the rapid rainshadow stream. It
surfaces in the center of the torrent, floating like a phalarope for a
moment before ducking back under. In quick little dives it is among the
stones near the far bank. Water sparkles like quicksilver over its dipping
head and neck. Watch for little fluttering wing movements when it dives,
for if you haven't seen them it will be hard to realize how this bird actually
flies underwater. Although closely related to thrushes, the Dipper
departs from a Robinlike appearance in special ways. Its large, strong
breast muscles and short wings, dense waterproof feathers, and strong
legs show how its body is adapted to its way of life. The sharp, clear call
of the Dipper rings out as its warm gray feathers and cold wet feet
become part of the stream once again.

Female Kokanee salmon in breeding condition

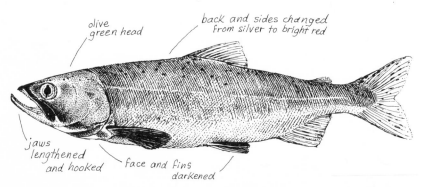

olive
green head

back and sides changed
from silver to bright red

jaws
lengthened
and hooked

face and fins
darkened

Red shimmers flash by you in the rippling, wavery, icy water, as small freshwater salmon passionately force their way against the current on a one-way trip. Milling about below each neck or dam, gathering strength from the substance of their deteriorating flesh to make the next leap, and hesitating in the lee of rocks, the bright fish pause before nosing up shallow riffles in the faces of the fastest flow. The sciences of current, resistance, and momentum are the links between their battered bodies and the perpetuation of the life of their kind. The ancestors of these fish have run this same stream for thousands of years, and they look and act as they do because they are the product of those that survived to spawn in this way. These are Kokanee, landlocked miniatures of the seventy centimeter Sockeye Salmon that run up from the sea to breed and die at the mouth of this stream. Sockeye breed in lakes and in the rivers near them, and schools of the young fish feed on planktonic crustacea and insects in the still, crystal water of the nursery lakes before descending the river to the sea. With such special feeding habits it is no surprise that wherever Sockeye occur, from Idaho to Alaska, to Siberia to Japan, there is also the little freshwater Kokanee which does not risk the long journey, trading fifteen-fold greater growth in the sea for the relative safety of the waters of a mountain lake.

Both males and females become red with green heads to spawn, and both are equally turned upon and gouged by the

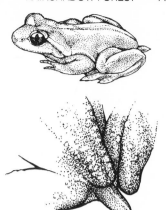

The male Tailed Frog, *Ascaphus truei*, has a "tail." Although its mating behavior is not well known, the "tail" is presumed to be for internal fertilization of the eggs of the female. Mt. Seymour, near Vancouver, B.C. 2 October 1976

The tadpole of *Ascaphus truei* has an enormously enlarged mouth with which it clings to rocks in the mountain torrents in which it lives and grows. Paleface Creek, near Chilliwack Lake, B.C. 18 September 1976

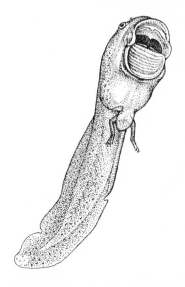

sharp teeth of their own kind. Fish with missing tail fins are especially noticeable, as their bodies wag ineffectually back and forth, as though flailing the air, meeting very little resistance from the water. The spent red fish, blotched with white fungus, have no self-pity and no feeling of well-earned rest after spawning, but struggle farther upstream until they lie flipping weakly against a root or a waterlogged branch, and soon die.

Yellowjacket wasps come to the carcasses. They don't mind close scrutiny as they work like busy butchers, cutting, with knifelike mouthparts, pieces of the white meat, just the right size to carry away between forelegs and under chin. They lift off, circle once, just above the fish to find their direction, and go off to feed their young ones in a paper nest underground. Don't leave yet. They will soon be back for more. I saw a wasp light near a murdered mosquito, ball it up neatly and fly away with a secure little parcel of meat.

Here in the lush green neighborhood of the mountain stream, standing in a grove of tall trees, it is easy to forget that you are in rainshadow. Just a few hundred meters up the mountain slope, the Ponderosa Pines, thin columns bearing round tufts of yellow-green needles, cast shadows on a tawny grass background, and beyond, the forest thins out on a jagged rocky peak against an empty sky.

Sharp-shinned Hawk

Pigmy Nuthatch

Nutcracker

Mountain Timberline

Timberline is the climate-imposed boundary beyond which trees cannot survive. The dry air, violent winds, and cold temperatures at certain altitudes and exposures create conditions in which only very low plants – if any at all – can grow. Observations in this chapter are based mainly on Mount Albert, Parc de la Gaspésie, Quebec; and Banff, Alberta.

High and remote from the world below, the mountain top rises naked above its forest-clad slopes. It changes its complexion with various lights and colors lent by the sky; now gleaming, snow clad in the clear winter sunshine; now darkening fitfully, with fast moving shadows, now ghosting in and out of view, bleak and gray amid masses of fog, or obscured in a turmoil of racing storm clouds. More than just a part of the sky, the barren treeless peak is as solid and real as the dark coniferous forest below.

Conditions vary among different peaks and ranges. The forest boundary occurs at a much lower altitude if the general climate is colder, drier, or windier. The altitude of timberline varies on individual slopes according to exposure and quality of roothold, so that small dark trees straggle up nearly vertical valleys and shadow the lees of minor crags. The rest of timberline is left below, at the bottoms of broad windswept rock faces and the vast, featureless steep-sloped fields of loose scree which are the trails of rock slides and avalanches.

Certain trees are better able to flourish in a cold climate than others. The forests just below timberline in the western mountains are composed mostly of Englemann Spruce and Alpine Fir, very like the boreal forest trees, White Spruce and Balsam Fir, which approach timberline in the mountains of the Gaspé Peninsula, Newfoundland, and Labrador. The mountains get more direct sun, and longer summers than the tundra does, so there is no permafrost. Treeline in the western mountains is characterized by special trees which work their roots deep into the rock, and can survive strong winds, dry weather, and severe winter. They are not found in the mountains of the east but, if they were, they might grow even higher than the existing timberline of White Spruce.

Rocky Mountain Bighorn sheep, *Ovis canadensis*

With long sweeping branches of short dense needle tufts, Whitebark and Limber pines grow upright where they are sheltered from the wind, but in exposed sites they cannot raise trunk or branches beyond the lee of a rock or boulder. The wind trains them to grow along the ground, where its speed is least, due to friction between the air and the irregular surface. The oppressed trees continually struggle to grow upward, but their trunks and boughs are bent down each winter by the weight of snow; and the branches that project above the drifts are subject to cold, and are blasted bare of foliage by swift, stinging particles of wind-driven ice. The low, rounded forms that remain produce needles and cones in the safety of numbers, offering little resistance to the wind. Pines that manage to grow upright in windy places seem to be only half there. They point downwind like flags or weather vanes, the leeward side of their trunks having full foliage, while on the side facing the prevailing wind no twigs can survive.

Alpine Larch is the hardiest timberline conifer species, clinging tiny, ancient, and gnarled to windswept slopes and crags as high as 2,300 meters above sea level. Alpine Larch, because its short, soft, blue-green needles turn yellow and drop in the autumn, does not lose precious moisture to the fast, freezing winter winds and its twigs are densely hairy to reduce moisture loss and to trap the heat of the sun.

Just as mountain timberline in the east has no tree species unique to high altitudes, its ground cover plants are those of the lowland tundra to the north. Wherever the deep snow melts early and there is roothold, Reindeer Moss lichen, pale and frothy, grows between stunted spruces, with dwarf birches and willows, and low shrub heaths such as Bearberry, Bilberry, blueberry, and Lapland Rosebay. Many special alpine plants

A timberline birch *Betula glandulosa*, with round leathery leaves and horizontal trunk, a little more than half a meter long. Alt. 1100 m, Mt. Albert, Parc de la Gaspésie, P.Q. 5 October 1977

live on the high slopes, peaks, and meadows of the western mountains. Cushion plants grow in dense low forms on the rock and gravel, like rounded patches of moss. Dark green and compact, they absorb the sun's heat, and keep it inside among many tiny, close leaves. This lengthens periods of warmth for, at high altitudes, night temperatures drop drastically, even in midsummer. There is little or no rain in the summer and many days of blazing sunshine, so cushion plants such as the Moss Campion grow very slowly, taking several years to establish a deep root system before flowering.

Some fragile alpine flowers begin spring growth underneath snow banks. The Snow Buttercup has been found ready to bloom while still deeply buried in snow. Protected from severe frost by the constant temperature of the snow, it melts water for its roots and room for its growth with the tiny bit of heat produced by its metabolism. It must be ready to produce seed during the short time that it may be free from snow cover.

Sedges, bunch grasses, and many bright wildflowers flourish in high meadows where water from melted snow is available for most of the summer. Here deep soil accumulates from minerals eroded from the mountain peaks and enriched by plant decomposition. Hoary-backed, rusty-bellied Columbian Ground Squirrels, which burrow in the meadows, graze above ground and may be seen sitting upright at their burrow entrances, basking in the sun. Long-tailed Voles inhabit old pocket gopher and ground squirrel tunnels. Burrowing mammals circulate the soil and improve the drainage of alpine meadows, having much the effect that earthworms do in soils of milder climates.

Mountain marmots make their tunnels among the large rocks of well-drained talus slopes. In the west live Pikas, guinea piglike rabbit relatives with large round ears and soft, thick fur. In summer they gather plants, dry them in miniature haystacks on rocks in the sun, and store them in dry places for food during the winter. Pikas are active all year round, and come above ground to bask even in winter. When they sense danger, they warn each other with sharp cries, their little bodies jerking forward with each explosive whistling bark, and then they drop quickly out of sight among the rocks.

Bands of Bighorn Sheep roam the peaks above timberline during the summer, browsing on the low alpine plants, and keeping a sharp lookout for danger. Their ability to run and leap on rocks is their defense, but Wolves can catch them in open meadows. Since the sheep are so wary, close observation is difficult, but it is possible if you approach them cautiously against the ground, from downwind so that they can neither see nor smell you. The usual view at close range is one of fleet and daring flight, surprisingly agile and surefooted over rough terrain.

A Gray Jay
in the rain

A great
collector of
anything
edible

Arbutus
menziesii,
the Pacific
Madrone
in Flower.
Evergreen,
its leaves
continually
grow and die

Notice
its dead
brown
leaves.

Arbutus

Arbutus menziesii *grows on dry sheltered slopes along the Pacific coast from California to British Columbia. Observations for this chapter were made at Little Qualicum Falls, Vancouver Island, and Horseshoe Bay, near Vancouver, British Columbia.*

There is a sheltered strip of partial rain shadow between the dripping rainforests of Vancouver Island and the Olympic Peninsula, and those of the higher Cascades and Coast Ranges. Forests of tall, straight, somber green Douglas Fir grow on the warm shores of the drowned valley that is Puget Sound and the Strait of Georgia. They are as regular as the telephone poles some of them may one day become. Below them, the ground is lacy with green-twigged *Vaccinium parvifolium*, the Red Huckleberry, with fruit like salmon eggs.

Orange among the straight dark firs writhe the fleshy limbs of *Arbutus menziesii*, sometimes called the Madrone. The northernmost broad-leaved evergreen tree and the tallest member of the heather family in North America, it seems caught in indecision. It has reached a tree's height by the twisted detours tracked by its crooked trunk, and only near the ground does it grow scaley tree bark of fawn, drab, or olive brown. The rest of the trunk and branches is soft and smooth like human skin, and sheds as if sunburned. The thin, hazel brown rind splits to reveal yellowish, olive green, or clay color underbark, drying into odd streamers and rolls, antique brown or tawny on the inside, chestnut, ferruginous, almost maroon on the outside, This rind falls in thin scraps to the forest floor with the oval leaves to join dry needles and bracted fir cones.

The peeling bark reminds you of paper birch, but the peels do not burn. Set fire to fallen *Arbutus* bark, and it goes out or smoulders. Touch the bark. It is soft and cool, smoother than any other bark. It flows rapidly across fire scars or carved abuse, obliterating carved dates only a few years old. The colors of *Arbutus* change with the quality of the light. They appear vivid among the greens at midday, rich-hued and moist in the morning mist, and burning like fire when the reddened light of sunset seeks them out among the trunks of the firs.

Saxifrage, *Saxifraga ferruginea*. Seaside cliffs, Bold Point, Quadra Island, B.C. 29 April 1977

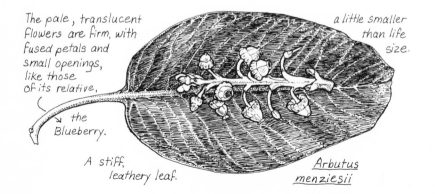

The pale, translucent flowers are firm, with fused petals and small openings, like those of its relative,

the Blueberry.

A stiff, leathery leaf.

a little smaller than life size.

Arbutus menziesii

Young Alder on an old fir stump

Sword Fern

Raspberry

Western Deciduous Forest

Second growth forests of deciduous trees have followed burning and clear-cutting of western rainforest throughout the Pacific Northwest. This chapter is based mostly on forests at Cultus Lake, Vedder Mountain, Quadra River, and Langley, British Columbia.

After the conifers were logged in the 1920s, Red Alders and Bigleaf Maple got a head start along with the showy, white-flowered raspberry and the pink-flowered Salmonberry; but there were few little firs, cedars, or hemlocks.

You can see far down the mountain under the green canopy. As you search for an easy path down the slopes, the rain-laden lacework of flowering plants soaks you to the knees. Sword Ferns reach to brush you with flat, tapered fronds of wetness. Across the dark old leaf litter are strewn long stems of bedstraw, strung with green asterisks of leaves, and flecked singly with tiny white flowers. There, *Rana aurora*, the Dawn Frog, sits upright, colored like a sunrise. It has a deep pink on its sides and underlegs, glowing into pale yellow and green where the hind legs

Monadenia
Fidelis

life size

often found in the
moist protection of
the big evergreen
fern, Polystichum

This large landsnail flourishes in the mineral-rich
litter of the Bigleaf Maple

fold against the body. It is a forest frog, with a brown, black-spotted back
to match the leaves when seen from above. Like the Wood Frog, it has a
black eye mask and white lip stripes.

Beware of Devil's Club, three meters tall, crowned by a spray of
giant maple-shaped leaves. The long, ungainly stem, at which you may
clutch for support, is thickly grown with long thin prickles that break off,
piercing your hands. Even the veins of the leaves of this well-protected
plant grow sharp spines, top and bottom. The stem changes direction at
regular intervals, marking each year's growth with a clublike hedge of
prickles. Now the new growth, splayed round by a fountain of
long-stemmed leaves, is spring green and bears a tall spike of nubbly,
pale green, fresh smelling flowers, aswarm with small foxy-colored
beetles, which are mating there as they pollinate the flowers.

The long branches of a Bigleaf Maple reach far from its trunk. In
spring, the massive trunks stand in a spacious glade, mistily carpeted
with delicate wildflowers, and dappled by sun and the light shade of big,
drooping leaves. These leaves will grow darker, spread, and stiffen as
the season progresses. The branches are muffled by lumps and heavy
sleeves of rich golden-green epiphytic mosses. Ferns glow from thick
wet nests of moss and from dark hollows and crevices in the bark.

After logging or burning in the western coastal forest the Red
Alder springs to a height of twenty meters in less than fifty years. It has
dark green leaves and brown cone fruits like other alders, but its trunk is
tall and straight, smooth and pale-barked. It is called Red Alder because
of the bright stain that seeps from the bark into the milk-white wood.
Paper Birches here look very much like this alder. Their reddish bark is
not shaggy and their leaves are rounder than those of eastern birches. A
few cedars and firs stand in this spring green forest, isolated or in small
groups, holding shadows close about them like cloaks.

A small gray movement flickers furtively at the edge of your vision
and, when you turn to look, a dead maple leaf rustles against another
where a Shrew Mole has slipped under cover. Its habitat is rich with
beetles, grubs, and earthworms to eat; these creatures in their turn
depend for their lives on the diverse plant community of the deciduous
forest.

A heavy bumblebee drones about her business among the

Bleeding Hearts. She brushes past leaves, scattering their burden of sun-sparkling raindrops, and bending the flower stalks far over with her weight; then she spreads the petals, probing the pale magenta blossoms for sweetness. She lands momentarily on a mossy stump and brushes the pollen from her body into the long basket hairs of her hind legs. She can work on cool, sunny mornings because her color is mostly black, which absorbs the sun's warmth, and her body is insulated by dense velvety hair, which holds the heat produced by her flight muscles. At the base of the stem of Bleeding Heart, just beneath the broad maple-shaped leaves of a young raspberry plant, a millipede crawls over a pillow of *Dicranum* moss. The yellow rectangles at the edges of each segment glow like the car windows of a railway train, as its body meanders on a multitude of tiny legs.

Just a random piece of dry Alder branch, not much more than a twig, left behind after its limb had been used for firewood. The smooth young bark is dry now, and a fine place for lichens to cover it like patchwork, flourishing various strange fruiting apothecia, all on the upper side, and all within a few years.

← 8 mm →

A big Black Bear walks across this glade nearly every day, headed perhaps for some tree that he likes to scratch his sides against. If he sees you walking here he'll turn and barrel off through the raspberry-choked hollow, across the stream and over a log into the shadow beneath the branches of a big cedar, his shiny black coat rippling. Then you may come down out of your tree and go to examine his tracks.

A slug of the genus Prophysaon

a groove around the body marks the point at which the slug constricts to drop its tail, an important adaptation because it forages at night, crawling into insect burrows in rotting wood to hide from the day, often getting grabbed by birds as it squeezes in at dawn.

On sunny banks of talus where raspberry, Oregon Grape, and Sword Ferns tangle at the feet of young alders and birches, little brown animals rustle mouselike, snakelike, through dry leaves and into crevices beneath sun-warmed shale. Alligator Lizards, *Gerronotus coeruleus,* are covered with an armor of close-fitting rectangular scales and have ears — holes in the sides of their heads — behind crafty, wrinkle-lidded eyes. If you catch one roughly, it will constrict special muscles at the base of the tail, and its solid little body will break nearly in half. The severed tail snaps and lashes, rustling dead leaves, putting up a much better show

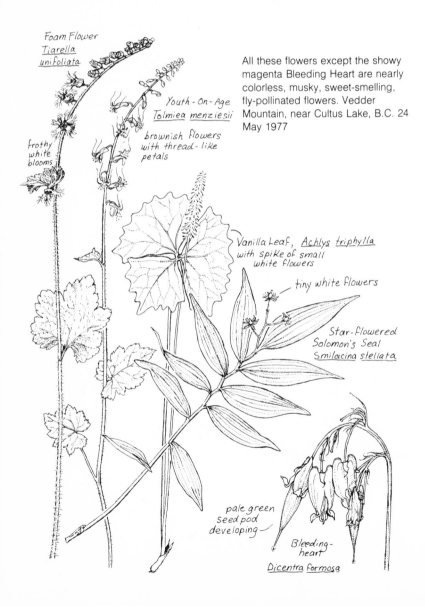

Foam Flower
Tiarella
unifoliata

frothy
white
blooms

Youth-On-Age
Tolmiea menziesii

brownish flowers
with thread-like
petals

All these flowers except the showy magenta Bleeding Heart are nearly colorless, musky, sweet-smelling, fly-pollinated flowers. Vedder Mountain, near Cultus Lake, B.C. 24 May 1977

Vanilla Leaf, Achlys triphylla
with spike of small
white flowers

tiny white flowers

Star-flowered
Solomon's Seal
Smilacina stellata

pale green
seed pod
developing

Bleeding-
heart

Dicentra formosa

Flying Squirrel,
Glaucomys sabrinus
oreganus

This shy,
quiet squirrel
glides from
branch to
branch
by spreading
the broad flaps
of skin between
front and hind
legs.

It eats
seeds, insects,
and sometimes
bird eggs,

and may be
seen at dusk,
as it sleeps
during the day,
and is active
at night.

Very little is known about the nesting and
breeding habits of this species.

The Shrew Mole,
Neurotrichus gibbsi,
is the smallest
North American
mole.

dense, coarse
slate grey
coat.

The eye is very
small, and serves
mainly to distinguish
light and darkness

the long,
flexible
nose can be
turned in different
directions at will.

body length,
6 to 8 cm.

than the whole lizard does. A predator is distracted by the tail while
Gerronotus sneaks away to grow another one. Most lizards lay eggs, but
Alligator Lizards hatch inside their mothers and are born in the autumn.
For generation after generation, Alligator Lizards spend long peaceful
summer days moving from cool dark tunnels onto warm flat rocks,
keeping their bodies at just the right temperature for efficiency as they
hunt millipedes, spiders, crickets, and other invertebrates, while the
deciduous trees which eventually shade the lizards out grow for another
season of their slow lives until they in turn are shaded out by the returning
evergreen forest.

Western Rainforest

Forests similar to those described in this chapter occur along the Pacific coast from Oregon to Alaska; they also occur inland, wherever mountains force the prevalent eastward winds to rise higher than they have before, and to drop their moisture as rain or snow. This chapter is based on forests near Tofino, Cameron Lake, Vancouver, and Mission, British Columbia.

As you climb up the bank from the road and come into the quiet of the western rainforest, you find yourself dwarfed in this great hall of plants. The lofty canopy with its tracery of black branches is as remote as the ceiling of a cathedral. The largest trees seem like walls, great slabs of bark, dark and damp to the touch, colored and textured by lichens and mosses. They tower in parallel bands to the sky, taking on the dimensions of landforms rather than those of familiar green plants.

It is dim in here. The colors that the plants use to make food have been filtered from the light by the forest canopy. In this diffuse green light the details of rock and bark, fallen fir cone, and lacy woodfern are crisp and clear. There is much darkness under tousled mats of overhanging moss and in the soft woody recesses of a crumbling log, but nothing casts a shadow. This quality of the light seems to take you into an underwater world. No breeze penetrates, but a faint and constant current gently nods the Sword Fern fronds, and the broad flat leaves of Vine Maple move softly. You feel a freshness on your face as the air of the forest follows invisible paths of convection like currents in the ocean.

young
Aneides
ferreus
under bark

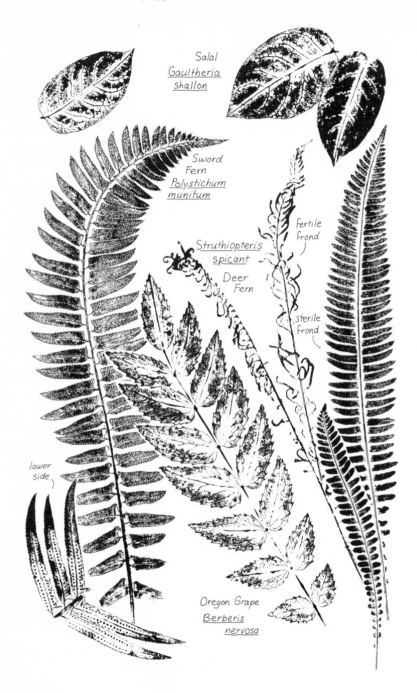

Salal
Gaultheria
shallon

Sword
Fern
Polystichum
munitum

Struthiopteris
spicant

Deer
Fern

fertile
frond

sterile
frond

lower
side

Oregon Grape
Berberis
nervosa

A *Trillium*'s white bloom is held aloft on a curving stalk from the junction of three large leaves. The leaves are soft, thin, and flat. They form a film of green, taking light from the triangular space they define. This is an extreme adaptation to growth in the shade. A single layer of leaf is spread like an umbrella to trap the light that has passed through the canopy above. Like the *Trillium*, young Western Hemlocks and Western Red Cedars on the forest floor turn single faces upward. Seen from above, their flat sprays and pleated sheets of foliage are woven into unbroken green. When these trees reach the canopy, their shape changes and the crowns are strung out loosely along the tall trunks, each layer casting only a light shadow on those beneath. The cedars change most, so that their own foliage hangs like moss from recurved limbs. Douglas Fir is intolerant of shade, and can begin life only where some disturbance has thrown down the forest. Its fluffy foliage of thin needles and hanging branches filters the bright sunlight into shade, gathering energy to propel the fir to immense height and meter-thick trunk in a century, and on to imponderable dimensions in its eight hundred-year natural lifetime.

Very few of the old unlogged western rainforests still exist. Walking into one, standing quietly between vast buttressed cedars or massive-trunked firs, think that these individuals were mature long before the first explorers wrote them into the history of North America. The trees tell time in their own quiet language of air, sun, rain, roots, and the thin ring of growth marked beneath the bark at the end of every cool, rainy winter.

Where there are many insect pests, the vegetation tends to be diverse, because solid stands of one kind of plant are easily infested. But the cool damp climate of the northern Pacific coast does not favor most insect life and predators of plants are scarce, so the largest trees, Cedar, Hemlock, and Fir, thrive undiscouraged and shade out all competiton.

The rainforest produces a climate of its own, free from the harshness of sun, wind, rain, and filled with plants that thrive on wetness. Algae, home of tardigrades and other myriad forms of microscopic life, films rocks and fallen branches with green slipperiness, and clots the water which drips down bark and down the sides of boulders from the ragged margins of the solid soaking moss, *Hookeria*. Liverworts, water-loving relatives of the mosses, plaster themselves, green and translucent, like seaweed, over wet rotting wood at the brink of a streamlet.

Sorex
obscurus,
the Dusky shrew.

life size

Living in stumps and logs, this quick little animal eats more than its own weight of insects and creeping things each day.

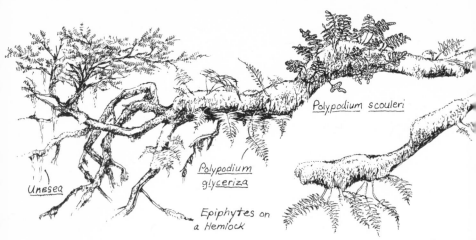

Polypodium scouleri

Polypodium glyceriza

Unseen

Epiphytes on a Hemlock

In February, while the cold Pacific rages in winter storms, the coastal valleys are evergreen with thick-leaved ferns and heaths. The far wall of the valley is ragged with scrambling Salal, nudging, crowding, standing on stumps, and even competing with epiphytic ferns up on the branches of trees. Versatile and ambitious in the pursuit of light and space, Salal's crooked, brown, smooth-skinned twigs thrust stiff oval dark green leaves everywhere. Among the Salal are *Vaccinium ovatum*, an evergreen blueberry with dark leaves like holly, and *Vaccinium parvifolium*, whose larger plants are ragged brooms of narrow, ridged green twigs, bare of their summer leaves, but whose lesser plants stay evergreen with small dark leaves seeking whatever light passes through the slightly thinner winter canopy. Clumped Sword Ferns droop last year's brown leaves beneath long green fronds, and the smaller Deer Fern flows down slopes and crowns stumps and logs, holding scraggly black-brown fertile fronds in the midst of silent fountains of compact, precisely formed leaves.

After a storm your path is littered with ruined lives from the tops of the trees: the greenish white of fallen *Usnea* in tangles of fragile softness, branches of fern, loose bits of moss, and flat hands of reticulated lichen, thrown down by the winds of a recent storm. Where huge trees have fallen, the old logs, shaggy and green, make a tortuous, undulating landscape over the forest floor. In places you may find a dark tunnel beneath a fallen giant preferable to a hard climb over it.

High on a steep seaside slope, you may have a better-than-ground-level view of a great old hemlock. A meter and a half in diameter, it is blanketed with unruly moss up to its ponderous blue-green crown. The epiphytic fern *Polypodium glycorhiza* grows on the dead branches and on thick places in the mossy coat, lending the tree an inner crown of bright grass green. In the low, tangled forest along the shore, it grows with leathery *Polypodium scouleri*, which is so tolerant of salt that it strays from the edge of the forest and clings in clumps to lichened rock walls and ledges in the mist of surf spray.

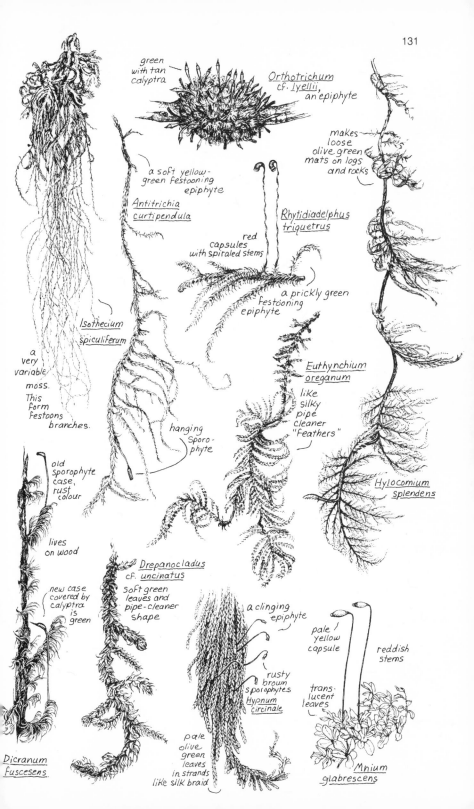

green with tan calyptra

Orthotrichum cf. _lyellii_, an epiphyte

makes loose olive green mats on logs and rocks

a soft yellow-green festooning epiphyte

Antitrichia curtipendula

red capsules with spiraled stems

Rhytidiadelphus triquetrus

a prickly green festooning epiphyte

Isothecium spiculiferum

a very variable moss. This form festoons branches.

hanging Sporo-phyte

Euthynchium oreganum

like silky pipe cleaner "feathers"

Hylocomium splendens

old sporophyte case, rust colour

lives on wood

new case covered by calyptra is green

Dicranum fuscescens

Drepanocladus cf. _uncinatus_

soft green leaves and pipe-cleaner shape

a clinging epiphyte

rusty brown sporophytes

Hypnum circinale

pale yellow capsule

reddish stems

trans-lucent leaves

pale olive green leaves in strands like silk braid

Mnium glabrescens

Rocky Intertidal

Rocky intertidal occurs wherever rock surface is exposed at the edge of the sea. It extends from areas which are occasionally wetted by waves, to those which are only briefly uncovered by the lowest tide. The west coast of North America is mostly rocky because of its folded coastal mountains. The east coast is rocky where the sediments overlying the bases of the old coastal mountain range there have been scraped away by glaciers. This chapter is based mainly on rocky shores at Rocky Harbor, Newfoundland; St. Andrews, New Brunswick; and Tofino and Quadra Arm, British Columbia.

The western horizon is restless with swells from storms far across the ocean, pushed over the sea in long, moving ridges. The rhythm of their approach changes as each wave finally trips on the shore, and on the backwash of those that have broken before. Rising to peaks, they fall headlong in a fury of white water, rushing to a thunderous impact on the obstinate rim of the North American Plate. The churning creamy surf writhes with internal violence. Leaping and dashing, it sprays erratic

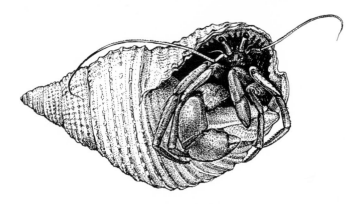

Hermit Crab, *Pagurus*, in Dire Whelk shell, *Searlesia dira*. Frank Island, near Tofino, Vancouver Island, B.C. 30 March 1977

white fountains as tons of water, possessed by the movement of the ocean, rebound from each contact with the immovable rock.

The bands of color on the wave-lashed flanks of the land are intertidal plants and animals mapping the conditions which are favorable to each dominant species. You can see that exposure to air is the most limiting factor because the lower zones follow the breaking waves up into cracks. Shining green Surfgrass *Phyllospadix* is combed straight by the retreat of each wave. Its roots pack tightly into cracks and its smooth narrow leaves offer nothing for the surf to break or tear. Around it on solid rock are kelps — tough, brown, and slippery. Some, like flexible miniature palm trees, bow down with each wave's impact and spring erect again; others, like frilled straps and broad ribbons, clutch at higher rocks with holdfasts that resemble tangled tree roots. Above is a broad, dark band of heavy-shelled *Mytilus californicus* mussels, large acorn barnacles, and raised clumps of goosenecked barnacles. All are able to close their shells to avoid water loss during low tide, and open them to feed when the water returns. Above them the small shining mussel *Mytilus edulis* forms a carpet with smaller acorn barnacles and short, dark golden tufts of frilly and beardlike algae. Highest of all, tiny brittle barnacles encrust bare rock in a light band just below a dark, black stripe of lichen and algae — the border between intertidal and terrestrial, the upper limit of the sea.

Sometimes exceptionally large waves are made by the joining of

Sharp-nosed Sculpin, *Clinocottus acuticeps*, when living in Surfgrass beds, is bright green. Frank Island, near Tofino, Vancouver Island, B.C. 15 February 1977

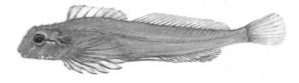

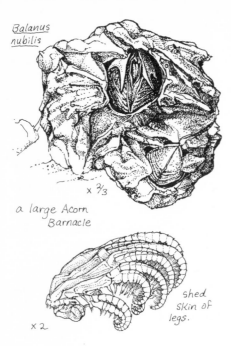

*Balanus
nubilis*

x ⅔

a large Acorn
  Barnacle

shed
skin of
legs.

x 2

two or more swells, unexpectedly drenching levels that had been dry since high tide. When exploring the water's edge, be watchful of the size of the swells and be ready to retreat. If escape is impossible, spread your body like a starfish, flat against the rock, and hold on so as not to be dashed against it or swept away.

As the tide rises, hermit crabs wedge themselves into cracks, and limpets, chitons, and topsnails clamp down tightly against the rock. Surfbirds fly up like a part of the spray as water collides with land. As you pick your way over one crest of rock and gaze at the face of another, a whole flock of Surfbirds may be there, like figures in an elaborate tapestry. Each is busy with its bill. You cannot see them all at once, and only become aware of the extent of the flock as you notice the movements of each bird. Probing with downcurved bill, a dainty, pale brown Rock Sandpiper feeds, looking, as other shorebirds do, like part of the rock itself.

If you sit still, and an Oystercatcher comes near to feed, you may see the bright red lids of its yellow eyes. I saw one Oystercatcher step with yellow legs over to a cluster of mussels, and its red bill was like a flame against the dark mussels. A few short jabbing and slashing movements into a slightly parted pair of valves, and the muscles which closed the shell were cut. The Oystercatcher had nearly a full crop with one big, soft, orange *Mytilus californicus* body. It retreated with quick steps from the splashes of a wave, and shook its head and tail before advancing again on the mussels and the large acorn barnacles, which grow on the mussel shells and in honeycomblike clusters among them. Barnacles are crustaceans, and their delicate sweet meat tastes like crab.

When the tide is high, the birds must wait on the windswept tops of capes and islands until their food source is uncovered once more. The small, black, Northwestern Crows, not much larger than Oystercatchers, retreat then to the beaches and the edge of the forest to look for carrion until they can return to the intertidal rocks to clean out mussel shells and pick up bits of barnacle.

The terrestrial flora begins above the band of lichen and algae-blackened rock which is reached by the sea only during storms. Tiny green, gray, and white lichens fleck the rock, and thin green algae seem to inhabit the very pores of the stone. Bent grasses and short dense mosses live with crisp, fat succulents, heaths, and other wind- and salt-tolerant plants, crowded into the cracks and crevices.

Hardy halophytic plants live in places like these at the edge of the northern Atlantic too. But below them, far down into the intertidal zone, the rock is bare of all sedentary life. In the more severe climate of this colder ocean, winter cakes the rocks with ice, and the jostling, crushing floes scrape the rocks clean of the thin slippery scum of greenish-yellow algae that grows during summer. Stout-bodied periwinkles and limpets stray far from cover on the exposed rock of the upper intertidal, to feed on this tissue-thin vegetable layer.

In cracks and crevices of the bedrock, and sheltered by vertical or undercut rock faces, tide pools are patterned by the rich brocades of the colors and textures of intertidal life. The sides of boulders are curtained by narrow, leathery branching ribbons of the brown algae *Ascophylum* with puffed, rounded, gas-filled bladders all along its length. Delicate tufts of translucent Sea Lettuce droop like wet green tissue but, underwater, they poise unfolded in brilliant bunches of graceful ruffles. Tough, frilly brown *Fucus*, with some lobes puffed out in nubbly bladders for flotation and reproduction, forms dense shaggy rugs over rocks, and underwater its thick bunches grow warmly with colors of wine, gold, and rust. Tide pool bottoms are blotched with

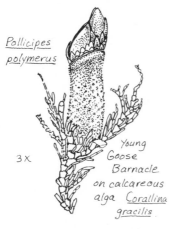

Pollicipes polymerus

3 x

Young Goose Barnacle on calcareous alga *Corallina gracilis*

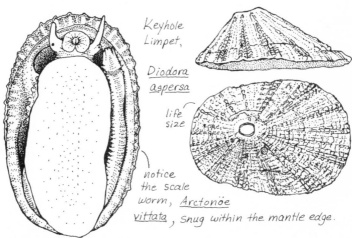

Keyhole Limpet,

Diodora aspersa

life size

notice the scale worm, *Arctonöe vittata*, snug within the mantle edge.

pink and white encrusting algae;
and Blue Mussels stand, singly,
like spring crocuses among
pebbles, or, where they are
grouped closely, like firm even
carpets, clinging to the stones and
to one another with strong elastic
byssus threads. Their fringed
mantles, pale or rich brown
according to where they live, line
the valves which, underwater, are
slightly ajar to filter-feed. Some
shells are brown with green rays,
but most are black and, where the
periostracum has been worn, the
shell beneath is chalky blue.

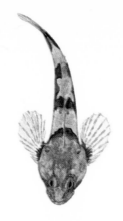

An eastern tide pool sculpin, probably
Myoxocephalus aeneus. Rocky
Harbor, Nfld. May 1976

Dark-colored shells benefit
intertidal animals, such as
periwinkles and mussels, which live in cool oceans. Dark surfaces
warm up quickly in the sun, enabling snails and limpets to creep faster
and eat more. Mussels eat by filtering plankton underwater. They digest
their food, grow, and prepare for reproduction more quickly as they bask
at low tide, dark-shelled, and vertically packed among their fellows. If
barnacles were black, those on exposed sunny rocks would be more
likely to overheat, dehydrate, and die, because they are fastened
permanently wherever they landed as planktonic larvae, but being
white-shelled, they can live in more exposed places, since they reflect
much of the sun's hot light from the
walls of their small ivory towers.
Young mussels also fasten
wherever they can, and you may
find them attached, like little black
seeds, among the high barnacles,
on slippery seaweed, or on
surf-battered boards. But mussels
can make and break their byssus
threads, and can cast themselves
adrift, or roam slowly across the
rocks until they anchor themselves
securely — usually among
countless other mussels who have
also found a place with the right
conditions.

Northern Clingfish, *Gobiesox
maeandricus,* attaches to the bottoms
of stones with pectoral fins modified as
a sucker. Raza Island, Strait of
Georgia, B.C. 4 May 1977

Sea urchins crouch, spiny,
on the pool bottoms. They are
never tolerant of exposure to air, or
even bright sunlight. Sometimes
you will find bits of broken *Fucus*

covering them untidily, pulled over and held there by tube feet for shade and camouflage. The slim, elastic tube feet, each ending in a round suction disk, are often beautifully banded in pink or red, and can extend past the spine tips. With them the urchin can walk surprisingly quickly. The disappearance of most seaweed below low tide level in areas where sea urchins are plentiful reflects the vegetarian habits of these squat, spiny ocean porcupines.

In well-protected parts of tide pools, *Metridium* anemones fasten like rust-colored volcanoes and spout clumps of fine brown tentacles. Some are closed tightly, limpet shaped, while some stretch up tall in tubes, and some are flattened widely like rubber tires. The mouth is a hole in the center, ringed with the fluid-filled tentacles. Sometimes there are crab legs or fish tails protruding from anemone mouths. Sea anemone tentacles have stinging cells called nematocysts, which stick to their prey, immobilizing it with poison. When touched, the surface of a tentacle will cling in a rather surprising way to a fingertip, but it cannot harm human skin.

In spring, the tide pools fairly twinkle with tiny orange, red, blue, or green flat-sided amphipods. They dash here and there, singles searching for mates, and pairs avoiding contact with others. The male's body arches over the back of the smaller female, clasping her tightly with legs specially shaped for the purpose, and the two swim as if they were one larger animal. A male amphipod will often clasp a female for days, risking predation to keep away other males, so that he may be present when she moults and is able to mate.

When the Atlantic ice breaks up and melts in the spring, small intertidal invertebrates move up out of cracks and from under rocks, and small fish, sea urchins, and seastars come up from deeper water into the sun-warmed tide pools. *Asterias vulgaris*, varying in pastel color through yellow, orange, pink, and brown, is the common eastern seastar.

The intertidal seastar fauna of the west coast is the richest in the world. In one place, you may find several species, ranging from the tiny blue and violet plaid *Leptasterias hexactus*, to the bright red-plated *Mediaster aequalis*; and from the soft-skinned, firm-bodied Leather Stars to the huge, flaccid, but agile Sunflower stars. Purple, orange, or brown, with blunt white spines, *Pisaster orchraceous* is the most abundant western seastar, and an omnipresent carnivore. Always eating something or going somewhere with seastar stealth, they creep so slowly that they are nearly sitting still. You may often see one grappling with a mussel, straining to insert its thin, transparent sack of a stomach between the reluctant valves, or approaching another starfish

Mossy Nudibranch, *Aeloidea papillosa* eats sea anemones

life size

which already is humped over a mussel. Limpets avoid them. Anemones ignore them.

The empty skeleton or "test" of a Green Sea Urchin

rows of tiny holes for tube feet

Knobs are the bases for spines

looking down on the underside, 5 strong sharp teeth meet out like fingertips, in the of water, life center of the the tube size mouth feet retract, *Strongylocentrotus* and only spines *droebachiensis* show.

Pacific tide pools have more species than Atlantic ones, probably because there has been more time and room for specialized intertidal species to evolve in the Pacific. On the Atlantic, relatively ice-free rocky shores extend only from Massachusetts to Nova Scotia, and this whole coast was recently buried under glacial ice; but the entire Pacific coast is rock, it was less glaciated, and the warm south-flowing Japanese Current makes conditions so uniform that many species are found from Alaska to northern Mexico.

There is only one kind of intertidal chiton in the east: a small, pink mollusc which lurks among kelp holdfasts in the deeper tide pools. Western chitons range through many sizes and colors. The wine-colored, velvety-backed, Gumboot Chiton lives beneath broad, brown kelp leaves; and the liquorice black midtidal *Katherina,* lives with sponges, anemones, and seastars on wet rock walls; and the small Lined Chiton, intricately scribed with red, white, and blue hair-thin lines, can be found among green surf anemones and calcareous alga, just below the lip of an upper tidepool.

At the bottom of this deep, clear pool grows a forest of tall, dark green Finger Sponge, gently circulating the water by beating tiny flagellae within its round stems and branches, filtering small plankton from the water. One by one, the flared crimson plumes of *Serpula* tube worms emerge from contorted white tubes, cemented to the vertical wall of the pool. They begin to feed, waving their tentacles in a circular motion, until you move and they all pop back inside.

In some pools, the movement of snail shells catches your eye, as topsnail, moon snail and large periwinkle shells hurry at a faster-than-snail's pace to escape the threat of your shadow or footfall. In tide pools with many hermit crabs, their social behavior is fascinating to watch. The main ambition of a hermit crab seems to be to chase every hermit crab that is smaller than itself. Hoisting its shell and scuttling over gravel and around rocks, a large crab forces a smaller one to dodge away, or to withdraw, cornered, into its shell. Then the large crab triumphantly clasps the snail shell of the smaller, discovers that it is too small for its own use, and goes off to conquer another. Sometimes, if the crabs are about the same size, they wrestle with one another, trying to tear off legs and claws. Usually, however, an aggressive gesture of white-tipped claws will result in the more timid of the two crabs giving ground. If a victor decides to claim a shell, the loser must vacate it, and then you will see its soft, defenseless abdomen, shaped to hook snugly inside a snail shell.

Some tidepools have no plants or animals clinging to their sides or bottoms — only round rocks and boulders which tumble and roll when the surf pounds into the kettlelike hole. The trapped boulders grind themselves down and enlarge their prison, while each tide washes away the sand they make. This is one of the few natural situations where there is nothing but rock and water; and the contrast leads you to consider how completely the rest of the world is covered with living things.

Small animals from floating seaweed near intertidal rocks. French Creek, NE of Parksville, Vancouver Island, B.C. May 1977

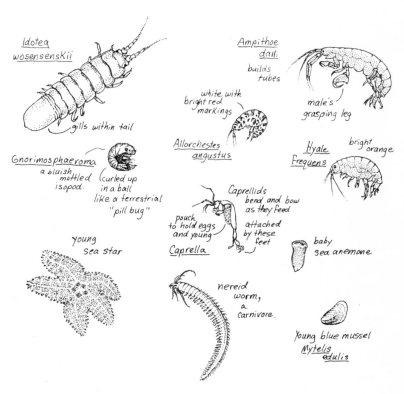

Idotea wosensenskii

gills within tail

Ampithoe daili
builds tubes

white with bright red markings

male's grasping leg

Gnorimosphaeroma
a bluish mottled isopod.
(curled up in a ball like a terrestrial "pill bug"

Allorchestes angustus

Hyale frequens
bright orange

young sea star

Caprellids bend and bow as they feed
pouch to hold eggs and young
attached by these feet
Caprella

baby sea anemone

nereid worm, a carnivore.

Young blue mussel
Mytelis edulis

ILLUSTRATIONS WITHOUT CAPTIONS

Note: Numbers in bold face refer to pages.

4 *Vitrina* snail on *Mnium* moss /Saskatoon Is. Prov. Pk., Grande Prairie, Alta. Aug. 1976. **8** Beach landscape with Sanderlings /Cap Lumière, Richibuctu, N.B. 13 Oct. 1977. **10** Bloodworm /Green Point, Pacific Rim Nat. Pk., Tofino, B.C. Feb. 1977; Gull tracks sand shrimp burrow, lugworm casting /Qualicum Beach, Vancouver Is., B.C. Dec. 1976; Olive Snail /Chesterman's Beach, Tofino, Vancouver Is., B.C. Mar. 1977. **13** Saltmarsh landscape with *Salicornia* /Cap lumière, Richibuctu, N.B. 13 Oct. 1977. **14** Bayberry and Beach Pea /Cap Lumière, Richibuctu, N.B. 12 Oct. 1977. **15** Eastern rainforest landscape /bank of Ste. Anne R., Parc de la Gaspésie, P.Q. 5 Oct. 1977. **16** Fungi of eastern rainforest /Parc de la Gaspésie, P.Q. 30 Sept. 1977. **18** Eastern rainforest lichens /Parc de la Gaspésie, P.Q. 1 Oct. 1977. **20** Starflower /Parc de la Gaspésie, P.Q. 28 Sept. 1977. **22** Eastern mixed forest and cleared land landscape /10 km W of Pugwash, N.S. 16 Oct. 1977. **26** Moth chrysalis /2 km N of Fredericton, N.B. 19 Oct. 1977. **27** Meadow Vole /Bishops Mills, S of Kemptville, Ont. 22 Oct. 1977. **30** Sapsucker-drilled maple bark /18 km E of James R., Pictou Co., N.S. 1 May 1976; Grouse droppings /Mark S. Burnham Prov. Pk., near Peterborough, Ont. winter 1975. **31** Mitrewort /3 km SW of Poltimore, Gatineau Co., P.Q. 19 July 1975. **32** Giant Puffball /Ottawa, Ont. 22 Sept. 1975. **33** Earthworms under oaks and elms /Scarborough, Toronto, Ont. Oct. 1977. **34** Great Lakes harbor landscape /Toronto, Ont. Jan. 1978. **35** Carp skull /Toronto, Ont. Nov. 1977. **36** City landscape /Quebec City, P.Q. Sept. 1977. **38** Leaf prints /Toronto, Ont. Oct. 1977. **39** Slugs and sowbug /backyard of house in Toronto, Ont. Oct. 1977. **40** Railroad embankment landscape /Canaan Station, N.B. 16 Oct. 1977. **41** *Draba*, a small mustard /Qualicum, Vancouver Is., B.C. 14 April 1977. **43** Purple-stemmed Cliffbrake /Rockwood, Ont. Sept. 1977; Pupillid snails /Portland, Ont. Nov. 1977; Spotted Camel Cricket /Ottawa, Ont. Summer 1975. **44** Orchid, Butterwort, watersnake, ribbonsnake /Dorcas Bay, Bruce Co., Ont. 17 July 1977. **48** Cedar lowland and stream landscape /Speed R., 2 km NW Oustic, Wellington Co., Ont. 30 Oct. 1977. **49** Poplar twig /Speed R., 2 km NW Oustic, Wellington Co., Ont. 10 May 1975; Crayfish, *Orconectes propinquus*, male, form two /Speed R., 2 km NW Oustic, Wellington Co., Ont. 30 Oct. 1977. **50** Life from a stone of the stream /Speed R., 2 km NW Oustic, Wellington Co., Ont. 31 Oct. 1977. **52** Cattail marsh landscape /Lake Scugog, near Port Perry, Ont. 4 May 1975. **53** Green Frog /Cicero Swamp, Onondaga Co., N.Y. Oct. 1975. **54** Muskrat, Blackbirds, bumblebee /Lake Scugog, near Port Perry, Ont. 4 May 1975. **56** Serfid fly larva and spider egg case, red velvet mites and beetle larva /Lake Scugog, near Port Perry, Ont. 15 April 1975. **58** Mollusc shells, springtail /Lake Scugog, near Port Perry, Ont. 15 April 1975. **59** Giant Water Bug /Oustic, Wellington Co., Ont. 20 July 1974. **60** Northern lake landscape /Harris Lake, Parry Sound Dist., Ont. 28 Aug. 1977. **63** Mayfly and spinner /Heronry Lake, 3 km S of Crow Lake, Kenora Dist., Ont. 20 June 1977; Rock Bass /Naiscoot Lake, Pointe au Baril, Parry Sound Dist., Ont. 26 Aug. 1977. **64** Quillwort /Rapid Pond, 7 km E of Pasadena, Nfld. 10 May 1976. **65** Bare rock shield landscape /Kaladar, Ont. **69** Jack Pine parts /Harris Lake Rd. and Hwy. 69, Parry Sound Dist., Ont. 28 Aug. 1977. **71** New burn /N of Opasatika, near Kapuskasing, Ont. 24 June 1977. **74** Bog closeup /20 km S of Cochrane, Ont. June 1977. **76, 77** Bog vegetation /Cap Lumière, Richibuctu, N.B. 11 Oct. 1977. **78** Tundra landscape /Coppermine, N.W.T. June 1975. **79** *Lupinus arcticus* /Coppermine, N.W.T. June 1975; Other wildflowers, northern Baffin, Is., N.W.T. summer 1972. **81** Jawbones. **82-3, 85-8** *Populus* leaves, grasses, caterpillar and pseudoscorpion, spiders /Saskatoon Is. Prov. Pk., Grande Prairie, Alta. Aug. 1976. **84** Western toad /by Waskahigan R., near Little Smoky, Alta. 9 Aug. 1976. **89** Wheat field landscape /from Hwy #1 E of Winnipeg, Man. 14 June 1977; Richardson's Groundsquirrel /10 km E of Medicine Hat, Sask. 8 June 1977. **90** Wheat grains /from farm near Brunkild, Man. 13 June 1977; Aerial view of farm /near Brunkild, Man. **92** Wild Oats /near Brunkild, Man. **93** Young Robin /wheat farm, near Brunkild, Man. 13 June 1977. **94** Avocets and Godwit /Grassy Lake, Alta. 7 June 1977. **95** Young *Pseudacris* /Oakbluff, Man. 16 June 1977. **96** Freshwater plants of prairie sloughs /Cypress Hills (western edge of eastern block), 9 June 1977. **97** Freshwater plants of prairie sloughs /N end of Pelican Lake, Ninette, Man. 15 June 1977. **99** Slough at sunset /Estevan, Sask. 14 June 1977. **100** Sagebrush Desert landscape /Similkameen R. valley 23.5 km W of Osoyoos, B.C. 29 May 1977. **103** Prickly Pear Cactus /from a specimen collected at Blind R., Souris Co., Man. 27 June 1889. **104** Tenebrionid beetle /Similkameen R. valley, 23.5 km W of Osoyoos, B.C. 29 May 1977. **108** *Selaginella densa* /42 km S of Lillooet, Fraser R. canyon, B.C. 1 Sept. 1976. **111** Ponderosa Pine rainshadow forest landscape /42 km S of Lillooet, Fraser R. canyon, B.C. 1 Sept. 1976. **114** Birds of rainshadow /S of Lillooet, Fraser R. canyon, B.C. 31 Aug. 1976. **115** Treeline landscape /near Banff, Alta. **118** Gray Jay /Mt. Albert, Parc de la Gaspésie, P.Q. 5 Oct. 1977. **119** Arbutus landscape /near Horseshoe Bay, B.C. 29 April 1977. **120** Arbutus leaf and flower /near Horseshoe Bay, B.C. 29 April 1977. **121** Young Alder on an old fir stump /Cultus Lake, B.C. June 1977. **122** Snail /Vedder Mountain, near Cultus Lake, B.C. 25 May 1977. **123** Alder twig /Vedder Mountain, near Cultus Lake, B.C. 26 May 1977; Slug /Salmon Valley, B.C. 25 Aug. 1976. **125** Squirrel and Shrew Mole /Cultus Lake, B.C. 15 Sept. 1976. **126** Western rainforest landscape /Davis Lake Prov. Pk. B.C. 20 May 1977. **127** Salamander and Cedar bark /Tofino Inlet, Vancouver Is., B.C. Feb. 1977. **128** Western rainforest evergreen undergrowth leaf prints /Green Point, Pacific Rim Nat. Pk., Vancouver Is., B.C. Feb. 1977. **129** Dusky Shrew /W end of Cameron Lake, Vancouver Is., B.C. 13 April 1977. **130** Epiphytes on a hemlock /Green Point, Pacific Rim Nat. Pk., Vancouver Is., B.C. 7 April 1977. **131** Western rainforest mosses /Davis Lake Prov. Pk. B.C. 19 May 1977. **132** Rocky intertidal landscape /Frank Is., near Tofino, Vancouver Is., B.C. 3 April 1977. **134** Acorn Barnacle /Frank Is., Vancouver Is., B.C. Feb. 1977. **135** Goose Barnacle and Keyhole Limpet /Frank Is., Vancouver Is., B.C. Feb. 1977. **137** Nudibranch /Qualicum Beach, Vancouver Is., B.C. May 1977.

INDEX AND GLOSSARY